FROM CRADLE TO STAGE

Stories from the Mothers Who Rocked
and Raised Rock Stars

VIRGINIA HANLON GROHL

CORONET

First published in Great Britain in 2017 by Coronet
An imprint of Hodder & Stoughton
An Hachette UK company

1

Copyright © Virginia Hanlon Grohl 2017

The right of Virginia Hanlon Grohl to be identified as the Author of the Work has
been asserted by her in accordance with the Copyright, Designs and Patents Act 1988.

A CIP catalogue record for this title is available from the British Library

Hardback ISBN: 978 1 473 63955 3
Trade Paperback ISBN: 978 1 473 63956 0
Ebook ISBN: 978 1 473 63957 7

Printed and bound by CPI Group (UK) Ltd, Croydon, CR0 4YY

Hodder & Stoughton policy is to use papers that are natural, renewable and
recyclable products and made from wood grown in sustainable forests. The logging
and manufacturing processes are expected to conform to the environmental
regulations of the country of origin.

Hodder & Stoughton Ltd
Carmelite House
50 Victoria Embankment
London EC4Y 0DZ

www.hodder.co.uk

For Lisa and David,
my very own superstars.

The first
chords

To music!

In the
spotlight

CONTENTS

PREFACE

THE LIGHTS IN THE ENORMOUS ARENA DIMMED. A thunderclap of one drum stroke. And then—the ROAR! The overwhelming surge of young voices screaming their acclamation for this exciting new band with the high-energy drummer. It was Nirvana, and the power hitter behind the drum kit was my son, Dave Grohl.

I held my breath. I knew nothing would ever be the same. That roar and that moment signaled the life change that propelled David Grohl from a musician in a van to the cover of *Rolling Stone*. The little boy who had pounded on homemade drum kits on his unmade bed and played his guitar to the records of Led Zeppelin and the Beatles was now on a big stage, masking his fright by frenetically pounding away. The music that had begun years before in a little suburban house in Virginia was now being heard throughout the world.

And I was the mother of a Rock Star.

Had I seen it coming? Of course not. But ours had always been a life full of music. I loved Motown and Mozart. My daughter, Lisa, collected a wide array of albums by Hüsker Dü, David Bowie, and Neil Young, to name a few, and shared them with us. And David's friends brought records from Metallica and Black Flag and other dangerous-sounding groups to our house. There was always music.

We sang together, most often in the car on long trips to visit grandmothers or out-of-state friends, those trips substituting for the vacations and airfares we couldn't afford. Today I would gladly trade a first-class flight to London for one of those happy, just-the-three-of-us car trips. We made up songs, we harmonized, we sang to the radio. And we played games, clapping the rhythm of a song for the other two to identify. Always music.

Sunday afternoons often found us at the jazz workshops at One Step Down in Washington, DC, a dark, smoky room where musicians in town for a Saturday gig would stop by and join the house trio. Everyone really listened there. No talking allowed. It was a gem of a place, now long gone but sorely missed.

I've often wondered about the mystical force that urges some of us to listen, to play, to sing, to surround ourselves with music. As time went on and I sat at the sides of larger and larger stages, I became more intrigued. I wanted to talk about it with some of the other mothers whose sons and daughters were sharing those stages. But they weren't to be found at the shows and festivals I attended.

Several years ago, at the New Orleans Jazz Festival, as I wondered aloud, "Where are they?" a friend said, "Go find them. You should write a book!"

So thanks to Jill Berliner, my "stop complaining and do something" friend, my journey began. Since then I've met remarkable women, all members of this special sorority of mothers of musicians. They have welcomed me into their homes, poured me cups of tea, and told me their stories. We have talked about the challenging energy levels of our supercharged progeny, the music lessons most of them rejected, the schools they endured, the paths they took. We've recalled the times and places that came before the fame, and the family histories that shaped the backgrounds of our beloved superstars. I have loved every minute of it.

I hope to share this collection of vastly different life stories with readers who are interested in the trials and joys of raising creative children and with those who are curious about how one generation's story forms the basis for the creators of the next.

Ireland

Mrs. O'Donoghue's B&B

Assisting at The Flying Saucer, Lisa's coffee shop

FOREWORD

by Dave Grohl

EVERY MUSICIAN REMEMBERS HIS FIRST LESSON.

That moment when you feel the spark of inspiration ignite, and your entire world catches fire. The rush of revelation. The earth-rattling epiphany that music is no longer just a sound, it's every breath you'll ever take again. A puzzle that you'll never solve, though you hold all the pieces. An addiction that you'll never kick, though you've been given the antidote. A religion that won't forgive, though it feels like heaven. That moment when you're handed the key to an alternative universe where everything is beautiful, everything is free, and nothing will ever be quite the same again. For some, the first day of the rest of their lives.

Mine? Well . . . there was no classroom, no conservatory. No sheet music or baton. No . . . It was in the front seat of a beige Ford Maverick, rolling through Springfield, Virginia, on a sweltering hot summer day in 1975.

My teacher? My mother. Ms. Virginia Hanlon Grohl.

I remember that drive to Pohick Bay, sun on my freckled six-year-old face, wind blowing through my shaggy hair as the legendary Carly Simon's "You're So Vain" played over the crackly old AM radio. My mother and I were smiling and singing along (as we always did) above the booming roar of the open windows, and as Mick Jagger's unmistak-

able voice joined the chorus . . . our voices split into harmony for the first time. My mother started singing Mick's lower line as I sang Carly's high lead vocal. Without realizing it . . . I was harmonizing! Just as they do in the song! My heart lit up! My eyes widened! And then something clicked . . . the sound of our two voices, singing two different melody lines, made me realize one of music's most basic principles: different notes, when sung together in harmony, create a chord.

This moment is burned in my heart and mind as my first love. It is the Michelangelo in my Sistine Chapel. My baptism. My musical "Big Bang," if you will. Hell, this was the chicken AND the egg! From that moment on, I heard life with an entirely new set of ears. I scoured the radio for harmony. I searched every record in the house to find more. Did every song have this amazing new trick I had just learned? Did everyone know about this? Had this been going on forever? Why hadn't anyone bothered to tell me?! Songs became more than songs; they became my toys. They became my puzzles. They became challenges and mysteries. Some became my best friends. Some became my worst enemies. I was fascinated, enraptured, obsessed! I was hooked!

That summer drive to the bay in our Ford Maverick took place over forty years ago, but that same feeling has never gone away. To this day,

Perfect harmony then...

and now

when the radio turns on . . . so do I. Music becomes my everything. I hear structure and composition. Arrangement and shape. Layers of rhythm. I hear the voice of an artist through his instrument. Stories without words. I can carry on a conversation with someone as I drive down the highway, but if there's a song on the radio, I'm probably more focused on the kick-drum pattern of the music than on what they're saying to me. Yes, it's that bad.

DNA is a miraculous thing. We all carry traits of people we have never met somewhere deep within our chemistry. I'm no scientist, but I believe that my musical abilities are proof of this. There is no divine intervention here. This is flesh and blood. This is something that comes from the inside out. The day I picked up a guitar and played Deep Purple's "Smoke on the Water" by ear, I knew that all I needed was that DNA and a whole lot of patience (something my mother clearly had an abundance of). These ears and this heart and mind were born of someone. Someone who shared that same love of music and song. I was blessed with a genetic symphony, waiting to perform. All it took was that spark. . . .

But beyond any biological information, there is love, something that defies all science and reason. And that, I am most fortunate to have been given. It's maybe the most defining factor in anyone's life. Surely an artist's greatest muse. And there is no love like a mother's love. It is life's greatest song. We are all indebted to the women who have given us life. For without them, there would be no music.

JOHN MICHAEL STIPE

Born: January 4, 1960, in Fort McPherson, Georgia

R.E.M. (1980–2011): Lead vocals

Genre: Rock

First Single: "Radio Free Europe" (1981)

First Album: *Chronic Town* (1982)

MARIANNE STIPE

Mother of Michael Stipe
(R.E.M.)

SEVERAL MILES OUTSIDE ATHENS, GEORGIA, in a rural area where houses sit far back from the road, I drove through the blazing autumnal canopy that surrounded the home of Marianne and John Stipe. There I was greeted by a woman with a slightly familiar face framed by curly gray hair. The resemblance to her son, Michael, was instantly apparent.

The house is small and cozy with an inviting screened-in back porch, a place to cool off on a hot Georgia day and look at the pond below. Antique church pews and an old merchant's table line the wall. It's a charming, relaxing spot, the one Marianne and John chose after years of moving from one Army base to the next.

Marianne and I headed for the kitchen table, where she poured mugs of hot coffee and served her delicious homemade coffee cake with Georgia pecans and crème fraiche. You just can't beat Southern hospitality. I had brought a copy of a 1992 *Rolling Stone* magazine with R.E.M. on the cover and placed it on the table.

"Oh my gosh," Marianne gasped as she saw the young faces of her son, Bill Berry, Mike Mills, and Peter Buck. "Look at them! They were like brothers."

She smiled affectionately at the memories that surfaced as I read aloud the *Rolling Stone* Music Awards Critics' Picks featured in that issue. "Best Album, R.E.M.; Best Single, R.E.M.; Best Band, R.E.M.; Best Singer—oh, he didn't get that."

"Van Morrison got it," she recalled instantly.

Michael & his sisters

(And then, an interesting addition: the Best New Band award that year went to Nirvana, the band my son played drums for.)

Marianne told me the story of her family, from her childhood days in Washington, DC, to her teenage years in Georgia, when her father's job as an auditor took the family to Atlanta. She recalled her college days at the University of North Georgia, where she met her husband, John Stipe, who was one of the six hundred ROTC cadets enrolled there. She laughs when she confesses her good luck at being one of the ninety-seven coeds in their midst. "I got a good one," she brags. "Fifty-eight years later, and here we are!"

From that point on the Army determined their destinations: Virginia, New Jersey, Georgia, Texas, Germany. The three Stipe children, Cyndy, Michael, and Lynda, were "Army brats" (though none lived up to the pejorative term) and spent their childhoods moving from base to base. "That's just the way life was," Marianne stated matter-of-factly. "They were normal kids who moved around a lot."

Sometimes Army life was challenging, especially during times of crisis, when world events created disruptions that Army wives had to deal with. Marianne learned to live with uncertainty, with fear, worry, and anxiety. But she accepted those aspects of the life she and John had chosen. There was no time to complain. She had children to look after. When Michael was three weeks old, John was sent to Korea for sixteen months. The man who returned was a stranger to his son, and there was a period of adjustment, of father and son getting to know each other. No long-term effects resulted, though. Michael and his father had a close relationship throughout the years that followed. When I met Marianne, Michael was fifty-five and spending most of his time in New York. She said he still spoke with his father on the phone almost every day.

The Cuban Missile Crisis of 1962 affected all the families stationed at Fort Benning, Georgia, where John was posted. For thirteen days the tension between the United States and Russia was heightened as the two countries came closer to nuclear war than at any other time in history. As it happened, I was also in Georgia then, living just off the Fort Benning post where PFC James Grohl was assigned to the Army newspaper. I taught English in a high school that had a mix of military and civilian students and teachers. Before news of the crisis broke, we had all witnessed trucks, tanks, jeeps, and railcars moving out of town. It was obvious that something was afoot, yet we weren't being told anything. When Marianne asked John if he would be leaving, he said, "If my toothbrush is gone, you'll know I've gone."

The confrontation between President Kennedy and Premier Khrushchev stemmed from the Russians' placement of missile facilities in Cuba, confirmed by an American U-2 spy plane. Khrushchev refused to remove them unless the United States agreed to take similar missiles out of Turkey, and the head-butting by two stubborn sovereigns began. It culminated in a tense naval blockade deployed to deter Russia from sending additional missiles to Cuba. As the enemy ships moved closer together, the Columbus High School students in my charge headed to our assigned bunker area, a janitor's room, to await the "all clear" on the intercom. Meanwhile, Marianne, at home a few miles away with young Michael and the girls, had to face the reality of an official "full alert." There were moments of panic when the question "What will we do?" had no answer. She was a military wife, learning how suddenly, how completely her life could be affected by world events.

The most difficult tests would come when John was sent to Vietnam—twice. Marianne was in Texas then, far from family, and she often felt alone. The children were in school, so they had busy, active days that weren't ruled by the constant television coverage the Army wives were drawn to. Military protocol required that Marianne serve as leader of the women in John's group, so she had to be there for them, offering support while meeting her own family's needs. It was a weighty burden. The worst days followed news of casualties, deaths, or the conferring of MIA statuses. Every day was a challenge.

In a recent conversation with Michael, I asked if he recalled that time. He was just a little boy then. Did he know how difficult the deployments were for his mother? He described himself as a very sensitive kid with "an antenna" that could read emotion. Not only did he understand his mother's fears, but he learned to respect the difficulty his father lived with as he went from war zone to family life and back to combat again. He guessed that the horrors his father witnessed would never be spoken about. And in a family that prided itself on open communication, they never were.

John's second "hardship tour" (a deployment that required the family to stay behind) to Vietnam was the most difficult. He was in hard combat every day, flying a helicopter that Marianne could identify by its insignia as she watched the interminable news tapes on television. The children were also aware and informed, although they didn't know at the time that John doubted he would make it out alive.

They watched growing demonstrations as the mood of the country became fractured and dissension replaced patriotism as a subject for reportage. Marianne is sure Michael was hurt to see the anti-Vietnam marchers' disdain for those serving in the war. "The children knew Daddy's boss ordered him to go because he was a serviceman doing service," she said. There were no major debates or discussions in the family then, just unease and the disquieting fears they had about whether and when they would see their father again.

Michael could sense the anxiety that silently blanketed them. Hoping to spare his mother, he recalls asking other adults around him to explain what was happening. His youthful empathy seems remarkable. He worried about both parents.

As it turned out, John defied all the odds. Despite flying into and out of hot zones every day, he was not injured. He came home with a knee injury from a volleyball game, his only painful physical reminder of that time.

Could the nomadic life of a military family have been significant to Michael's choice to become a touring musician? The life of a military "brat" meant constant challenges in the form of new cities. New countries became the next stopping place, the next home. Marianne says that as time went by they all got used to it, even enjoyed it. She got better at it. At first she found the task of packing and unpacking for a family of five a daunting exercise. "And then I got to the point where I just let the Army come in and do it for me." As a result, she recalls her surprise at unpacking a kitchen box that revealed a half-eaten, month-old birthday cake that had been left on the counter. The movers, instructed to pack everything, had not forgotten a crumb.

In the mid-1960s the Stipe family moved to Germany, where they were posted in Hanau, outside Frankfurt. Visiting the Saturday markets, eating and learning to cook German specialties, and exploring their environs in a vintage VW fostered many family memories. On day trips the kids clamored to play their favorite game. "Mama, let's get lost! Let's get lost!" Ah, those nostalgic pre-GPS days when one could set out to bravely conquer untrodden roads. The kids were at just the right ages to appreciate all they saw, and the German people were welcoming. Marianne loved shopping there. Her husband teased her that *"Wie viel kostet das?"* ("What does that cost?") was the only German she mastered.

It was in Germany, at the home of a babysitter, that Michael recalls his first musical memory. It was the Beatles song "Michelle" playing on an old radio on a tall shelf. His memory is visual; he watched the radio dial as the song played. It didn't change his life.

Michael hadn't seemed destined to become the unique, charismatic rock star that we know. His mother says he was "high activity, maybe what is labeled hyperactive now." He was curious about things and channeled his energy by applying himself to tasks creatively and with determination. He wouldn't stop until he had finished something. He and his sisters liked to sing together, but their songs were from musicals or children's shows, not rock anthems. Michael took piano lessons and when he was in third grade learned to play the accordion as well.

When Michael was in high school, though, he began to listen to and read about the new sounds emanating from the New York music scene. At the age of fifteen he bought Patti Smith's first album, *Horses,* on the day it came out and stayed up all night listening to it. He "decided then and there that that was what I was going to do," he said.

That was life changing.

A life change was also in store for John and Marianne. After twenty-six years of Army life, John retired, and they were finally able to choose where to live. They chose Athens, home of the University of Georgia, and Michael joined them there when he decided to transfer from his Illinois college. That decision became the preface for this entire story. On that Georgia campus, where hundreds of bands formed and disbanded at an astonishing rate, R.E.M. was born.

In the 1970s the University of Georgia in Athens was emerging as the home to a unique music scene. Students were thirsty for beer and hungry for music, and nobody was stopping them from sating those appetites. The warm Georgia nights drew kids to outside shows, where hundreds gathered around kegs and listened to groups that may have formed that same week. It was open season all year round.

The B-52s were the first notable group to come out of the scene. Their fresh take on song styling was just what their young audiences wanted: catchy tunes that invited wild, energetic dancing.

It was during this time, between 1978 and 1980, that R.E.M. "happened." First Michael Stipe met Peter Buck, who was the manager of the record shop Wuxtry Records, a popular Athens gathering place for lovers of all kinds of music old and new, even some not yet getting radio play. It was the old-fashioned kind of record store where collectors and fans congregated to listen to albums they dug out of racks. Michael and Peter became friends and decided to start their own band. When a friend introduced them to Bill Berry and Mike Mills, the rhythm section completed the group—as yet unnamed. Michael was the singer, Peter Buck the guitar player, with Mike Mills on bass and Bill Berry on drums.

They lived in a musty old church—drafty and rat infested, according to Marianne. It's been torn down, but the steeple remains an Athens tourist attraction. It was there on April 5, 1980, that the newly named R.E.M. played their first show to an enthusiastic audience of five hundred. Michael, microphone in hand, seemed to come alive, feeding on the energy in the room, whirling, moving eccentrically in bursts of frenetic motion. Suddenly the band was talked about, written about, and asked to play bigger shows—for money!

The rapid success of the band led Michael to invite his parents for dinner at a Mexican restaurant, where "the conversation" took place.

"I want to drop out of school for six months," he said, "to see what this band will do. If nothing happens, I'll go back to school."

Michael remembers how frightened he was to present this scenario to his parents. He knew how hard they had worked and how much they had sacrificed to raise the money to put their three children through college, and he feared that his decision to go out on the road with a new band seemed like a pipe dream. He also remembers that their response was "instantly, incredibly supportive."

"They were almost Buddhist in their reaction, so in the moment," he recalls. "They said, 'Pursue your dream; see where this goes. If you have to go back to school, you can go back to school.'"

So it began. From 1981, when they released their first single, to 2011, when they disbanded, R.E.M. was one of the biggest bands in the world. They sold tens of millions of records and won many awards: two *Billboard* Music Awards, two Brit Awards, numerous MTV awards, and three Grammys (out of fourteen nominations). In 2007 they were inducted into the Rock and Roll Hall of Fame.

Marianne and John loved going to R.E.M. shows and joined them on their last European tour, traveling to festivals and arenas on tour buses with the band. This rock mom loved everything about it. She walked

Virginia & Marianne

The Athens Steeple

from tent to tent at the festivals to hear new bands as well as headliners. She fearlessly went out front when R.E.M. took the stage so she could absorb the full experience, feel the crowd's excitement. Later she would find her safe, comfortable backstage spot.

From these vantage points she gained a true appreciation for her son's gift as a front man. "He's a Southern gentleman," she says. He is genuine in acknowledging that if it weren't for those audiences, he wouldn't have the benefits his amazing success has brought him. She also realized how hard everyone worked onstage and off. To a casual fan it might appear as though a few hours onstage is an easy day's work. To those who understand the stresses of travel, the long periods of preparation, the grueling schedules, and the unending demands of the press and the public, it is clearly exhausting.

Michael was not surprised by the joy his mother experienced on their European bus tour. He describes her as "vivacious, very alive— a thrilling person to listen to, talk to, bounce ideas off." And he loves that she has always been curious and incredibly interested in the world around her, always learning and growing beyond the ideas of the generation she inhabits.

He always felt supported, understood, deeply loved. He wrote an untitled song for his parents that's about their staying up late to watch him on TV performing somewhere halfway around the world. He described it as being "like a beautiful little prayer":

I've seen the world and so awake
(Keep him strong)
And stay up late to hear me sing
Just hold her
I've seen the world and so awake
(Keep him strong)
And stay up late to hear me sing
Just hold him

Marianne is touched by other R.E.M. songs, too, including "Leaving New York," "Find the River," and "Everybody Hurts."

John Stipe passed away in 2015, about eight months after I visited Athens. Before he became ill he had finished a series of horticulture classes and encouraged his wife to go through the Master Gardener program, an intensive four-month course. They became committed organic gardeners and spent many hours together defying the stubborn red Georgia clay and producing great harvests of vegetables and flowers.

When I visited them, a Southern-style Thanksgiving feast for twenty-five was being planned. Black-eyed peas, sweet potatoes, greens, and corn pudding would accompany the turkey. "Michael always brings kale and chooses the best cheeses," Marianne said. Perhaps they would recall their greatest food memories, like cooking with Mario Batali on a trip to Venice. Michael's friendship with the famous chef resulted in a Mario-Marianne bond when she helped him prepare tortellini. Now she regularly sends Batali jars of her homemade pear relish, made from a recipe that's been passed down in her family for a hundred years, and she sees him on her trips to New York.

When R.E.M. disbanded Michael began to explore other aspects of his creativity. He made large bronze animal sculptures and revived his long-held interest in photography, a passion he shared with his father. He is currently working on a video installation for an exhibition planned for 2017 as well as on a book of photographs that he says is somewhat autobiographical. He feels "a compulsion, a need" to create; he believes that is the way of the artist. The woman who many years ago inspired him to take this path, Patti Smith, is now a close friend, one whom he still finds "astonishing."

Before I left Marianne and their warm, comfortable home, she and I talked about an event that brought both our sons together, the 2015 Rock and Roll Hall of Fame Induction Ceremony. She had been proud and I had been moved by Michael's quiet eloquence in the induction speech he gave for Nirvana. He spoke of the band's "indelible legacy," describing it as "capturing lightning in a bottle." He elaborated on Nirvana's importance to their particular time in history "by acknowledging the political machinations of petty, but broad-reaching political arguments, movements, and positions that held us culturally back. Nirvana blasted through all that with crystalline rage and fury." In a somber aside, he made special note of "that voice, that voice. Kurt, we miss you."

It was honest, poetic, moving, philosophical, beautifully true.

VIGNETTE #1:

THE CONVERSATION

Conversations, those brief moments we share with others, are rarely recorded, saved, or even noted. Much later, with the perspective of time and, yes, wisdom, we begin to understand which ones were most significant.

Among those that loom large in my life is the "dropping out of school" conversation. The dedicated schoolteacher mother and her beloved, brilliant, but unscholarly teenage son faced it head on.

"I want to tour with Scream," he said.

Scream, a seminal DC punk band, was a major force in the local music scene that I had become closely acquainted with. The leader, Pete Stahl, is a handsome, charismatic bundle of energy. But more important to me was the way he looked after his much younger drummer. I liked him, I trusted him, and I closed my ears to all the questions I knew would arise about the value of this raw, cacophonous music. I had gone to more than a few of their shows and I was pretty sure they wouldn't replace the Beatles.

But they had something. It was energetic, exciting, and loud, unlike anything I had ever heard. And David loved it.

What David didn't love was school. Early on I believed that his intelligence and creativity would be sparked by a teacher or class or program that would engage him. But it was not to be. Despite the fact that we lived in an area served by a nationally regarded school system (of which I was a part), there was no place for him. He failed to thrive in classroom after classroom. His teachers liked him, the kids liked him, so socially he was a hit. But dismal conferences and report cards showed his lack of academic connection. When I was appointed to a countywide committee to craft a program for the Gifted and Talented, before the first meeting had ended I understood that the capital *G* and *T* simply dressed up a program for academically adroit students, kids who probably didn't need much more of our help. And that's what it became.

I have often regretted that I didn't fight for my son, but, like him, I was beaten down by a system that served most people well. So it always seemed

10

to be "our fault." This pattern of disappointment made the dropping-out-of-school conversation a short, happy one. Touring the United States and Europe provided the opportunity for an education that going to another American History class or doing another math assignment couldn't compare to. I thought it was a great idea. I was sorry I couldn't go along.

Few parents understand that way of thinking, but I'm guessing that the mothers of many rock stars and artists nod their heads in recognition. The schools have failed some of our children; it's not the other way around.

So off he went. He toured the United States and Europe, spending his late teens in New York, Chicago, LA, Amsterdam, London, and Paris. The band members put thousands of miles on an old white Dodge, slept on friends' floors, and ate a lot of fast food. The van broke down in every other state, and a member of the band who had a troubled history with drugs and women landed in jail or in hiding a few times. (I can laugh at some of the stories now as they are revealed; others may never be confessed.)

It was when the Troubled One was MIA and shows in California had to be canceled and they were broke and helpless that David was invited to audition for Nirvana in Aberdeen, Washington. Shortly after David joined Nirvana they signed with DGC Records and became the biggest sensation in music in decades. They changed the course of popular music in the very short four years they existed as a band.

And my son had become a rock star!

When the dropping-out-of-school conversation started, neither of us dared to imagine that the outcome would be so exciting and life changing. I could have said, "Just go to school, get your education, have something to fall back on. Not many people make it in the music business."

But I didn't. Because even then I knew that some do.

Touring with Scream

Scream
l to r: Franz Stahl,
Harley Davidson,
Dave Grohl,
Pete Stahl,
Skeeter Thompson
(seated above)

ANDRE ROMELLE YOUNG

Born: February 18, 1965, in Compton, California

Dr. Dre (1992–present), World Class Wreckin' Cru (1984–'85), N.W.A (1986–'91): Vocals, synthesizer, keyboard, turntables, drum machine, sampler

Genre: Rap

First N.W.A Album: *Straight Outta Compton* (1988)

VERNA GRIFFIN

Mother of Andre Young
(Dr. Dre)

THE *LOS ANGELES TIMES* REPORTED that June 19, 2014, was celebrated as Dre Day in Compton, California. A photograph shows hundreds of teens wearing Dr. Dre T-shirts as they gathered to honor their
hometown hero, who had become Compton's first black billionaire. Dr.
Dre, born Andre Young, had grown up in their neighborhood and had
made them proud, first of his music, and now of his incredible success
as an enterprising businessman.

Forty-nine years earlier, on another June day in Compton, the four-
month-old Andre was being cradled by his mother as she looked out on
the flames beyond her window. Compton was a war zone, ablaze with
the Watts riots of 1965. Verna was a teenage mother, living with her parents, a seventeen-year-old husband, and her new baby, reading baby-
care books and hoping for a bright future. Then the world around her
exploded into chaos. Outside their walls whole blocks were on fire. Businesses were being looted. Martial law was declared. What had begun as
a dispute over a traffic stop on a hot summer night ended five days later
after activating over thirty thousand angry rioters and resulting in over
three thousand arrests, thirty-four deaths, and $45 million in property
damage. It was part of a rebellion that was sweeping the United States,
with almost every major city experiencing race riots that year.

It also led to the emergence of new voices in an expanded political
and music scene. The Black Power movement, the Black Panther Party,
and other forces raised issues that had fueled the riots as our country

struggled to come to terms with disparities in housing, employment, basic rights, and opportunity. This was Dre's birthright, which he would translate to the underlying themes of his lyrics years later when he became a part of the hip-hop group N.W.A (Niggaz With Attitude) and shock the music world with a hit rap song, "F_ _ _ tha Police." Dre then worked his way through an emerging rap scene in roles ranging from performer to producer to entrepreneur. How had this child become a headline-making billionaire? How had he gone from the arms of a frightened young mother to the *Forbes* list of the World's Most Powerful People?

For the answer, or some part of it, I decided to go to the original source and set out on a sweltering California morning to meet Dre's mother, Verna Griffin, in her beautiful suburban Los Angeles home. I was met at the door by a tall, very youthful woman who welcomed me in and led me through her house to a kitchen table, where she poured tea, placed a plate of just-made sugar cookies before us, and told me her story.

I had read *Long Road Outta Compton,* Verna's autobiography, published in 2008. In it she tells the stories of her sharecropper grandparents in Texas, her parents' struggles in Southern California, and her own journey from childhood to parenthood. It's a compelling tale.

Verna is proud of her enterprising grandparents. Looking back, she sees the lessons they left for their family as they translated their lives, limited by long-held practices of segregation, into a kind of prosperity not often achieved by those in their situation. They defied expectations by taking ownership of a sugar mill, becoming completely self-sufficient on their piece of land. Her grandmother sewed all the clothing for her nine girls and two boys, a talent that has extended across the generations to Verna, who outfitted the bride and all fourteen attendants at her daughter's wedding.

Verna was born on February 4, 1949, in Long Beach, California, to a single mother, Roberta, who worked in a factory making men's trousers. A year after Verna's birth, Roberta married Matthew Silverson, who adopted Verna and moved his family to Los Angeles. Both parents worked long hours, so Verna spent her early years at the home of a stern, abusive babysitter, coming home only on weekends for wonderful reunions with her family and a backyard full of friends. It wasn't until she was in

Verna & Dre...

Family celebrations

the third grade that her mother discovered the scars that revealed that Verna was being mistreated and immediately brought her home to stay. Verna had been secretive and uncomplaining because she was worried that the blame for the beatings would be placed on her. She had already learned to be wary, tough, and resilient, traits that would serve her well later in life—and that would be emulated by her first son, Andre.

Alternately a devilish troublemaker and a popular, engaged student, Verna experienced successes and failures. At one point she was expelled from school; at others, she was thriving and winning awards. In ninth grade she and several friends formed a singing group, the Four Aces, and enjoyed entertaining at neighborhood parties. At the same time, some boys in the neighborhood formed the Romells. Theodore Young, a tall, well-liked seventeen-year-old boy, was the leader of that group . . . and Verna fell madly in love. And got pregnant. At fifteen.

So after ninth grade Verna became the wife of Theodore and the mother of Andre Romelle Young, known to us now as Dr. Dre.

For a brief time, life in Verna's new family was fine. Theodore got a good job, and they were able to move into a two-bedroom house. As she devoted all her time to Andre, she discovered that her baby hated quiet. He would cry if there was no music or noise around him. Verna made sure the house was filled all day long with those great 1960s tunes. The year of Andre's birth was the year of the Four Tops, the Temptations,

Marvin Gaye, the Supremes, James Brown, the Rolling Stones, and the Beatles, among others. The music had a soothing effect on Andre; he would listen until he fell asleep. Verna built an extensive record collection and a few years later encouraged Dre to be their miniature DJ when friends came over. By then, he knew all the records by their colors and designs even though he could not yet read, and he loved spinning them for company. "It seems that he was born with a love for music," Verna said.

All these years later, Dre, at fifty-one, still spends a lot of time listening to Curtis Mayfield, Barry White, and Marvin Gaye, his all-time favorites. It's '70s rock and soul that he most loves. "That's what gets me going," he says.

All was harmonious in Verna's life until Theodore lost his job. The dangerous options for making money that their Compton neighborhood offered were a source of worry to Verna. Fiercely protective of her son, she would move out, going to her parents' house with Andre, when their arguments became heated. But Theodore would beg her to come back and she often gave in, hoping for the best for all of them. It was during this unsettled time in 1966 that their second child, Jerome Le-Vonte Young, was born. When he was just a few months old, he died in his sleep, apparently of a type of undiagnosed pneumonia. The young mother was devastated. Andre was confused and saddened by the loss of his "Bubby." Not long after that, Theodore was arrested and jailed and Verna, finally free of abuse and fear, filed for divorce. At eighteen she found herself back home with a child to care for and support.

Verna recalls that Andre was a very friendly baby who always seemed to be in a hurry. He grew fast and walked early, never pausing for the crawling stage. Because she had to work he spent most of his time with his grandparents and became very attached to them. His grandmother began teaching him poetry when he was three. Verna probably wonders now if his talent with words and rhymes began in that early period of his life.

The next years brought many changes. Verna married Curtis Crayon, who was a father figure to Andre. When she gave birth to Tyree, Andre happily took on the role of big brother, helping with diapers and feedings and lovingly holding the tiny child with whom he would create a lifelong bond, the brother he would call his best friend.

Verna expected Andre to be helpful, well behaved, and respectful. She observed that he "seemed to have a grown-up sense." Her expectation of a successful marriage, on the other hand, was dashed when Curtis proved to be inconsistent. Although he sometimes seemed to be a caring parent, she could not accept the unpredictable nature of his treatment of her. She still had hopes that her own high standards would be the ones that would be influential in her children's lives. Verna also endured the tragic death of another son, who was born prematurely and survived only two days. She had lost two children before emerging from childhood herself.

Verna, Curtis, and their sons moved often as Curtis went from job to job. Then Verna and Curtis divorced. There were several attempts at reconciliation and another child, a girl this time. Shameka Denee Crayon was born in November 1976. After Shameka was born Verna began to work at McDonnell Douglas, a major aerospace corporation, as an operations control analyst. That job would last thirteen years and finally provide a modicum of security for the woman who wanted little more than a safe, stable home for her children.

By now Andre was eleven, doing his best to "take on the responsibilities of a man," Verna says. She had been strict with her children, expecting them to do chores, to keep the house neat and clean. They had schedules and rules, one of which was to make sure she knew where they were at all times. When they wanted money "for fancy shoes or the latest thing," Verna assigned extra duties, often asking her own parents for lists of chores they needed to have done. Andre learned early to respect the things he had and to work for the things he dreamed of. Verna takes pride in this. "They grew up knowing they had to earn their own way."

Andre's early years were spent being shuttled from his home to his grandparents' house to babysitters as Verna took whatever job she could. Like Verna had, he spent weekdays with his grandparents and was returned to Verna for weekends. It wasn't what Verna had hoped for; she felt guilty. But she had no choice.

Verna had hoped that her serious, rather introverted son would succeed in school. He seemed to have learned the disciplines of respect and responsibility at home, but when embarking on junior high school Andre needed her encouragement. Because he was so quiet and kept his problems to himself, "I had to pay close attention to him to know if something bothered him. He just wouldn't say," she told me.

His teachers began calling, complaining of truancy, of his lack of interest. His grades dropped. Verna often went to his school for conferences, hoping for a solution. Dre had begun to imitate his mother's pattern of excelling in the classes he liked (math, drafting) and failing the rest. Despite her efforts at "calmly counseling him," he got As and Fs.

When Dre and I recently spoke, he talked about the mother-son conflicts that arose during that time. "I really didn't like school," he said. "I started having a lot of problems in junior high. I was going because I had to, not because I felt like I wanted to. I had other interests. I knew what I wanted to do with my life at a young age—and it's what I'm doing today."

Dre issued his declaration of independence at age fourteen when he fell in love with DJ'ing. "It's so prominent in my memory I remem-

Verna at home

Verna & Dre
do Christmas

ber the exact moment," he recalls. He was at a friend's house and for the first time heard a DJ scratching records on a song by Grandmaster Flash. "What is that? I wanna learn how to do that! This is what I'm gonna be doing!" He taught himself the skill using makeshift equipment, borrowing what he needed to build his own kit.

"And I've been doing the same thing ever since," he says. "In retrospect, it's like I'd been being trained to do what I do since I can remember." Even before age fourteen, he was "honing in on the craft just by listening and trying to understand who was doing what."

He had found his instrument. It wasn't the equipment he had built. It was his ear. He could hear nuances in sound, varieties of rhythm, new harmonies, and structures. He combined them and built new compositions from them. He could hear what others could not.

A few years later there was another problem. Verna's handsome son discovered girls much too early. Verna advised him to be careful and tried to get one girl's mother to intercede when it was clear the young lovers were spending too much time together. Their talks did nothing to quell the teenage passions, and at seventeen Andre was the father of baby LaTonya, making Verna a grandmother at the ripe old age of thirty-three. There was no talk of marriage. The young mother's family wanted Dre to stay away and not even see the new baby. But he managed to visit secretly, and Verna bought gifts for her grandchild. Before long, they all went their separate ways for many years.

There were other lessons to be learned. A gang culture developed rapidly during the chaotic breakdown of social structure that followed the Watts riots. Young, impressionable kids aligned themselves with Crips or Bloods, perhaps for the acceptance and belonging that all children crave, or for the camaraderie and sense of power that membership in a group would provide. Some of them may have thought that the benefits of monetary gain outweighed the loss of safety inherent in gang life. Knowing full well that those dangerous influences lay right beyond their doorstep, Verna showed by example that in order to make things better you don't waste time blaming the world around you. You find a way; you figure it out. And then you work harder than anyone else until you achieve something.

"She's been that way my entire life," Dre says. "She will not stop. She's an amazing woman, you know. I get a lot of inspiration from her."

Dre was one of the few who could maneuver his way through the treacherous social maze without affiliating himself with gangs. He was able to withhold his allegiance to Red or Blue without offending either side as he opted to wear black. A quiet, astute observer of his surroundings, he wanted more than the dangers and complications of a thug lifestyle, more than the dead-end jobs and sad lives that Compton offered. He wanted to make money. And he wanted to do it with music.

In 1984 Verna bought her son the Christmas gift he had been begging for: a mixer, a device that would combine recorded and live sounds to create new music. It would allow Dre to take the old '60s tunes he had grown up with and rough them up a bit, creating a new platform for the rhymes he sang over them. "That was the holy grail for me," he says.

He formed a group called Freak Patrol and got a job at Eve's After Dark, a nightclub where he worked on weekends. It was there that Dr. Dre, the Master of Mixology, was born, making fifty dollars a night. Verna drove Tyree and his friends to the club every Saturday at nine and returned to pick them up at one a.m. Those young fans witnessed the beginning of the careers of Dr. Dre, Ice Cube, and N.W.A. Dre was on his way.

*   *   *

People often ask music moms like Verna and me if we really like the music our sons are making. Some sneer as if to say, "Oh, c'mon, you can be honest with me," and don't believe me when I say I love Foo Fighters music. Have they not heard the throbbing melody of "Everlong"? Have they not come to tears listening to "Times Like These"? Or laughed at the bouncy jazz in "For All the Cows"? I could go on and on.

Perhaps, though, there's a greater challenge for a mother of a rap musician. Accusations of misogyny and the glorification of violence often accompany the question here. When told Dre's group would be called N.W.A and an early release would be "F_ _ _ tha Police," Verna was taken aback. Her son had avoided street life, the thug society. But let's be honest; he grew up in Compton, where being profiled was a constant and expected way of life. So when Verna listened, really listened, she heard the truth that lay beneath the curses and the shock.

She agreed with her son's description of this new genre as "reality rap" not "gangsta rap." She remembered the injustices she and her sons had observed and experienced, and she tried not to worry about what the reaction would be to this in-your-face music.

It was powerful. Young kids, black and white, reveled in the rebellious messages that outraged authorities and parents. Police forces geared up to handle anticipated violence at shows. Albums wore stickers that said everything but "censored." The lyrics were aggressive; the language was "street." The subjects were police brutality, guns, women, sex, money. It's easy to understand Verna's misgivings. The songs were a far cry from the Motown melodies she had played for her son.

With the wisdom of age Dre looks back on their first record and realizes they may have been reckless with lyrics that demeaned women, but back then they didn't think about that. "We were just kids having fun," Dre says. He is quick to point out, though, that the powerful political statements N.W.A made "still resonate today. I think we were on point."

The thug life came even closer to home. Although Verna and Dre had warned that wearing the blue or red of the Crips or Bloods would surely bring trouble, Tyree insisted he could do as he liked. And he liked red pants. One afternoon as she waited for her son to come home from middle school, Verna heard her name being shouted from the end of the street and looked out to see Tyree being pursued by a gang. He was running for his life. As he slid in the door, Verna grabbed the nearest weapon, a brass umbrella stand, and began screaming and swinging away, fending off the dangerous (and incredulous) crew. The offending pants went straight to the trash.

But Verna's moment of victory was brief. Although Tyree was the first in the family to graduate from high school, he was a constant worry to Verna, and when he was killed in a confrontation with a gang member, she was undone. All those years of being supportive and protective were overshadowed by the dangers that had always surrounded them. Dre canceled a tour and came home to mourn his brother. Verna, who had always been the strong one, was nearly broken. Perhaps it was counseling, or more likely it was Cedric, Tyree's year-and-a-half-old son, that helped her find something to live for again. Verna took guardianship of the child while his mother served out her assignment in the

Navy, and somehow Verna became Verna again. "She's one of the strongest women I've ever known," her son says, noting that her whole life has been spent enduring and getting past painful times.

The 2015 film *Straight Outta Compton,* which tells the story of N.W.A, heartbreakingly depicts the scene of Dre's return from his tour after receiving the news of his brother's death. He sobs uncontrollably at the loss of "my best friend" and blames himself for leaving Tyree behind. Verna's first instinct was also self-blame, and in the film we see their strength shift back and forth as each tries to convince the other to move beyond the blame. We feel their utter devastation and sense the deep love of family.

Dre was twenty-four when Tyree was killed. It had been a life-changing year for him as he had become the biggest star in rap. He was now very rich. And he worked all the time, early to late every day. For a while, when Verna wanted to see him, she had to go to his studio or his performances.

Dre did, however, invite his mother to see the first home he purchased, in Agoura Hills, a small, affluent city just outside LA. He has been financially generous with her, helping her start several businesses and bailing her out when they weren't successful. He bought her a new Mercedes and a house and arranged things so she would "never have to see a bill." Dre told me he's trying to be as good a son as he can be. "I took my mother through a lot of problems through my teenage years, so I have a little bit of making up to do."

Still, Verna sought to lead an independent life through her own creativity. She went back to her sewing machine to create fashionable outfits for a boutique that didn't succeed and later honed her craft by creating authentic African fashions for men and women and holding style shows to exhibit them. She had prepared for those enterprises by enrolling at the Fashion Institute of Design and Merchandising, where she studied textiles and pattern making, competing with much younger students. Dre encouraged her to follow her dream. Perhaps he remembered how she had made all his outfits for elementary school and for his short-lived dance career when he and his friends competed in pop-lock contests, and the wedding garments she'd made for so many family members.

Verna and her son are still round-the-clock energy machines. Dre, who began his career with shocking views of violent street life in Compton and had an early association with the notorious Suge Knight of Death Row Records, went on to form his own record company, Aftermath Entertainment, and to forge a remarkably successful career. He moved from rapping to producing and has worked with Eminem, 50 Cent, Jay Z, and many other top names. He won his first Grammy in 1994, with many others to follow.

In 2008 Dre and Jimmy Iovine created the company Beats by Dre, the premiere headphone maker. At forty-nine he became the second-wealthiest hip-hop artist on the *Forbes* Five list based on a net worth of $440 million. In 2013 Dre and Iovine gave USC a $70 million gift to create an academy for arts, technology, and the business of innovation.

When released in 2015, *Straight Outta Compton* received critical acclaim. Dre and Ice Cube served as producers on the project, making sure the casting and writing reflected their harsh reality. The violence, danger, and manipulation that the young innovators endured are excruciatingly played out, and the film has been nominated for dozens of awards, including several from the Motion Picture Academy and the Screen Actors Guild. There should have been more.

As a follow-up, Dre released *Compton: A Soundtrack by Dr. Dre*. He has said the album was inspired by the movie and that he plans to donate royalties to the city of Compton for a performing arts facility.

Verna is portrayed in one short scene in the film as the angry, disappointed mother who faces the departure of her son as he moves out to make music his life. She slaps him, then watches him walk away. The actress who portrays her is chic and good looking—an accurate portrait, I thought.

I asked Verna what it was like to see herself depicted on the big screen. She said it was strange, but she thought the scene captured that defining moment. She thought the entire story was truthfully and beautifully told.

Verna is secure now in a beautiful home, caring for her eighty-five-year-old mother, spending hours at her sewing machine working on her new product line, and staying involved with the school activities of her fifteen grandchildren and nine great-grandkids. She recently finished

Creative Verna with stained glass...

and in culinary arts

writing a 263-page book that details and honors the legacy of her family. She designed box covers for the book and gave copies to all the family members at a recent reunion of the ever-expanding clan.

As I was leaving her home after a lovely afternoon of conversation, Verna and I walked through her dining room. Laid out on the table were paper patterns and hundreds of pieces of colored glass next to a completed stained-glass sconce, a current project she hadn't even mentioned. When I expressed my amazement to Dre, he chuckled knowingly. "She's always just doing something artistic," he said.

The year 2016 was significant for Verna. The fashion line she had been working on for two years, Modern Mod Fashions, was finally up and running as an online boutique featuring attractive casual wear—jackets, leggings, and vests with colorful mixes of solids and bold patterns. Nowhere on her website is mention made that she is the mother of Dr. Dre. "I want my fashion to sell my name," she declares, "not my name to sell my fashion."

Andre had a busy year, too. After the success of *Straight Outta Compton* there was a surge of interest in N.W.A. The Thirty-First Annual Rock and Roll Hall of Fame Induction Ceremony featured the four surviving members accepting their award. Ice Cube, their spokesman, assured the doubters in the audience that their hip-hop band was indeed rock and roll. "Rock and roll is not conforming; it is outside the box, and rock and roll is N.W.A." Dre remarked that the success of their band should send a message to kids in places like Compton that "anything is possible," a lesson he shares with his own children. He has been married to Nicole Threatt Young for twenty years.

A month later N.W.A appeared on the main stage at the Coachella Festival, marking the first time the group had performed together in twenty-seven years. Some said it would probably be the last.

What we know is that it won't be the last we'll hear of Andre Young. His determined, nonstop work ethic has made him a model of success in music, business, and beyond. In 2017 Dre will branch out even further when he appears on *Vital Signs*, a six-episode original TV show from Apple, which he cowrote and produced. He's been training in acting to prepare for this role, which is loosely based on his life, he says, and he's very enthusiastic about it. "It's a great transition for my career," he says, "something different, a new way of creative expression."

Although Verna finds herself having to "counsel him to get some rest," she applauds his perseverance. Her less-than-subtle gift of a sleep-number pillow has probably not changed his workaholic nature, but she knows why. The woman who ambitiously started a new business at sixty-seven firmly believes that "everyone has a purpose and we should not remain stagnant. We may take a break, but as long as you have breath of life, there is no stopping."

In addition, when Verna views all her son's successes, she says, "I feel like I, too, have accomplished something. That's what I wanted— for my children to grow up and make something of themselves, to do better than me. That makes me very proud."

MIRANDA LEIGH LAMBERT

Born: November 10, 1983, in Longview, Texas

Miranda Lambert (2003–present): Vocals, guitar, keyboard, piano

Genre: Country

First Album: *Kerosene* (2005)

BEV LAMBERT

Mother of
Miranda Lambert

MIRANDA LAMBERT'S KEEPER OF THE FLAME tour set fire to the Greek Theatre in Los Angeles on a balmy August evening in 2016, and I was fortunate to be there to feel the heat—and to meet the gun-to-tin' singer who brought it. She was warm and funny backstage, then exploded into full "here's my story" mode when she stormed out to greet her audience with "Fastest Girl in Town." She followed that with a mix of songs that displayed heartfelt lyrics about a woman's journey. About independence, heartbreak, despair, hope, and deep reverence for the past. She's a brilliant storyteller and a fierce performer. It was a great show.

But I knew it would be. Bev Lambert, her mother, had told me what to expect when I visited her in Lindale, Texas, last year. She had invited me to meet her at the Pink Pistol boutique, a destination point for Miranda's fans from all over the country. After turning off the highway where a huge billboard picture of Miranda announces the shop, one enters the screen door to find pink pajamas, mugs, sequined denim, cowboy boots—and lots of Miranda posters. Bev, the merchandise manager for her daughter, engages each fan in conversation while they're there, and the shoppers leave with bulging bags and contented smiles. They've had a good time.

The drive to the Lambert home took us way out in the country to a large farmhouse with a barn and outbuildings. Several rows of carefully tended grapevines lined the driveway, where two shiny Airstream trailers were parked next to several small cars. No Lamborghinis or Ferraris or even fancy trucks in sight. Chickens and dogs scattered as we walked to the front porch of the house, where Rick Lambert, Bev's husband (and Miranda's dad), welcomed us. Then he excused himself to head to the kitchen to prepare our lunch, "a special Texas treat," he promised with a sly smile.

Bev told me how they met. When she was fifteen, she attended a cheerleading camp at Southern Methodist University, in Dallas, and caught a glimpse of her dream man, a handsome, self-assured fellow. She told her mother she was certain she would marry him. Unfortunately, he was twenty-four, much too old for her, and was on campus in his capacity as an undercover narcotics officer.

But he was unforgettable. A few years later, after her freshman year in college, Bev searched him out, invited him to coffee to congratulate him on his recent engagement—or so she said—and they have been together ever since. The Dallas cop—the guy who worked cases in homicide, vice, and narcotics—and the pretty young cheerleader who tracked him down formed Team Lambert, a partnership that would have them working together for years into the future in ways they could not have imagined.

Their first collaborative effort was a private investigation company. The Texas oil boom of the 1970s and early '80s had created a newly rich, entitled class of professionals—doctors, athletes, lawyers—who spent their money freely. The occasional dalliances that accompanied prosperity often put their reputations and finances at risk, so it was prime time for savvy snoops to either keep lids on or blow them off. Rick and Bev were very good at their chosen profession. Bev found the outrageous behavior of some of the overpaid athletes she investigated particularly offensive and went after them gleefully.

By the time Miranda was six or seven, she, too, was part of the team, brought in on special cases. One case involved a wealthy doctor's philandering wife who was spending most of her time at their posh resort condo with her young daughter. The husband suspected an affair and hired Bev and Rick to find out. Rick donned a floppy hat and Hawaiian shirt and lurked among the dunes with his camera and binoculars to do the necessary surveillance. Bev charmed her way past the "Members Only" gates, befriended Madam X, bought her margaritas, and

Bev & Miranda...   enjoying happy times

waited for the whole lurid story to pour out into the recorder (which, by the way, was in her beach bag. It's tough to wear a wire in a bikini). Just to make sure the encounter wouldn't be questioned, Bev had instructed Miranda to look for the woman's daughter at the pool and play with her. "As a little joke," Miranda was to tell her new friend that her mommy was a teacher. (Teachers are harmless. You can trust a teacher.) The woman's tale of betrayal detailed her passionate affair with a much younger man who turned out to be an international drug dealer.

Another caper involved dressing Miranda in a junior-high cheerleading costume and sending her out "selling candy for the school" so she could look for the incriminating evidence her parents needed. According to Bev, Miranda was never suspected and never had to appear in court because no one ever made the connection that she had provided information.

The oil crash that devastated the Texas economy at the end of that prosperous decade brought everyone down. The Lamberts had built a new house, had two children, two cars, dogs, and some livestock. Things were looking good. But they lost it all. Their phone stopped ringing. It was a sad, bleak period. To start over they moved to Lindale, a small town chosen by Bev for a school system she admired. Bev wanted her children to experience stability and permanence. She rented some farmland to hold the livestock they had accrued and enrolled Miranda in the first grade. The children and the animals would be fine. Rick, on the other hand, would not. He was a broken man, Bev said, whose ego was unable to withstand the beating it took when his successful enterprise and enviable income diminished. He regularly made the long commute to Dallas to look for work, but he sank into depression more than once.

Every day, Bev took Miranda to school then returned to the farm to feed her animals. As she walked the land she prayed, "God, give me the ground under my feet." They rented a tiny, rat-infested house that they fixed up in an attempt to make it a livable home for themselves and their two children until Bev could have the house of her dreams, a big, white house with wraparound porches that fronted an old sugarcane farm. "I would pass it every day and pray, 'God, I need you to let me have that house.'"

Only a few months later Bev was amazed that her prayers were answered when an old man in overalls appeared on her porch. "You that lady that drives by the white house on the hill every day?" He had noticed how nicely she was fixing up her sad little rental and offered her the dream house for less rent than she was currently paying if she would help renovate this much larger farmhouse with the inviting porches.

"He was a preacher and he heard from God," Bev said. She had found "a place to come home to," as Miranda described it. The singer who has traveled the world views Lindale as her "solid foundation, the kind of town that stands for something, where people get behind you."

After settling into a quieter life in Lindale, their case of a lifetime came along. Bev and Rick were hired by the lawyers for Paula Jones to investigate Bill Clinton. For two and a half years they traveled to meet people who would help them build a case. Some spat on them. Many feared any kind of involvement in a case so public and politically charged. But the Lamberts created massive files, which they stored in their Lindale home.

That arrangement led to some very strange events. As Bev tells it, she was in the backyard hanging laundry one day when she became aware of a helicopter circling overhead. A helicopter in Lindale was most unusual, and the fact that it seemed to have zeroed in on their property alarmed her. She ran to the phone to call Rick. He instructed her to get his binoculars and read the registration number on the copter's tail. When she told him there was no number, his voice tightened. "Listen to me, and listen to me good. Get every file on our property, every single document, every tape, every shred of paper, and your computer. Take everything we have to a safe place, and don't tell me where it is."

According to Bev, a subpoena was served, and those files became a crucial part of the Clinton impeachment investigation. "It was Ken Starr's people calling, ripping my files off. That's what he presented to the House managers." This strange tale of intrigue marked the end of their investigation, but it has provided Bev with dozens of stories that I'm sure she'll tell in her own book someday. Like her daughter, she is a natural storyteller.

Years later Team Lambert switched the family business from private investigations to music management when it became clear that their teenage daughter was supremely talented and ready to go on the very hazardous road that is the path to country music fame. Miranda's first performance of note had been when she was in the third grade. Accompanied by Rick on guitar, she sang "Daddy's Hands" in a talent show. At the end of the song she put her tiny hands on his, a sweet, touching gesture.

There was always music in the Lambert house. Rick had been a songwriter and guitar player in a country band. Bev had idolized Carole King and Merle Haggard. Bev describes the young Miranda as extremely shy. She loved to sing and enjoyed learning her daddy's songs and singing along with him. But she thought she would grow up to be a choir teacher, a safe choice for someone who found getting on a stage alone in front of an audience a frightful prospect.

However, one day when she was around sixteen, Miranda was listening to her radio while doing yard work when she heard an ad for the True Value Country Showdown, a talent show for kids in that part of Texas. She threw her rake to the ground and ran to the house. "I'm gonna enter that show, Mom!"

And she did. As she sang some of Rick's songs, the shy little girl "just came alive onstage," Bev said. "She didn't win, but she heard the applause and she couldn't get over it. That was it. That was the day."

Miranda finished high school early, and off they went. Rick and Bev began a new career, booking gigs and managing their talented country-star-to-be. They spent three thousand dollars making a CD and hit the road looking for radio stations and dive bars, where Miranda would play for free just to get someone to listen. Bev says she stalked the Texas artists Pat Green, Jack Ingram, Cooder Graw, and others and urged them to consider booking Miranda to tour with them. "Look," she'd say, "why would you want another 'hat act' with a ball cap or a Stetson, another one just like you, when you can get a girl? You might win a few fans with her."

That approach seemed to work. Rick bought a motor home. They painted cowboy hats and decorated them with bottle caps and made five hundred dollars per show selling them. Gas money! They were falling behind on their bills but were committed to Miranda's career.

"My dad and mom treated my music career as my college," Miranda explains. "They put money they didn't have into guitars and equipment and trudged through the beginning stages, the hardest ones, with me."

There were challenges. The strong-minded mother was managing and booking a teenage daughter who was eager to be independent. Bev admits she was "working out of her skill set," and the two faced their biggest mother-daughter conflicts during that time. "It was near catastrophic to our relationship," Bev remembers.

But Miranda gives her mother credit for wrangling audiences and filling rooms. She tells me how hard both her parents worked on those early tours. "My dad drove the 1985 Coronado motor home. He sold merch and set up the stage, then tore it down and packed it in the trailer. My mom booked my gigs. She drove me all over Texas to radio stations and auditions. She gathered people to come to my shows" so Miranda wouldn't feel as though she was playing to an empty room.

Then *Nashville Star* came along. It was a new television show that everyone thought would be country music's answer to *American Idol*. Miranda went to Fort Worth, Texas, to audition—and bombed. "She sang the wrong song, she had the wrong outfit, she had the wrong demeanor," Bev said.

Bev was beyond disappointed. She was furious. "You know what, Baby?" she scolded, "I'm killin' it for you. I'm killin' it. I'm twelve hours a day, balls to the wall. I'm giving you the best I've got. That wasn't even close! You go back. You go try it again. We're going to Houston"—for the next audition—"and you're going to try like you mean it. And if you don't make it, I'll never say another word. But don't you half-ass me. I'm not half-assing you!"

Miranda remembers that tough love. She wanted to make her own way but "through all of that she pushed me, and I'm glad she did. She said, 'If you want it, go get it and stop whining.' So we did. We did it together."

In Houston—with the perfect hair, the perfect demeanor, and the perfect outfit—Miranda sang the perfect song, Patsy Cline's "Crazy," and brought the house down. As the competition narrowed she seemed to learn about holding an audience. She didn't win but she was spellbinding. And people noticed.

Then it was off to Nashville. She had just turned eighteen and was on an airplane for the first time. She got a manager and a record deal, and her fourteen-year-old-brother, Luke, proved to the astonished business pros that he was an apt choice for webmaster. Bev was able to step back a bit but continued to be in charge of merchandise and the fan club. Of course, some were critical of all the family involvement and cautioned Miranda that her parents might be too embroiled in the business. Her reply: "Hey, when they start doing a bad job or get in the way, we'll fire 'em."

"So it was easy," Bev says. "We just stayed out of the way and did a good job." She is now in partnership with Miranda in six companies. She is also the ever-worried mom who sends her daughter vitamin drinks and reminds her to get more rest. And she makes sure Miranda remembers birthdays and anniversaries. She also sings a few lines of "Button Up Your Overcoat" at the end of her calls to both children, couching her motherly concerns in the melodies of an old standard.

She says they think she wrote it.

When Rick called us to lunch, the handgun that had been on the kitchen counter when I arrived had been replaced by steaming bowls of Texas taco soup made exotic by the addition of eland meat. Another unfortunate member of the eland family was mounted on a wall in the TV room, its tightly curled antlers reaching from the knotty-pine paneling. The meat and the soup were delicious, by the way. Chef Rick talked for a while about his love of hunting and the places he'd like to travel to, then laughed when he realized his adventurous tales were being told by a man in an apron. "I really am macho!" he protested, chuckling.

Rick has stepped back a bit from his early van-driving, merch-selling, roadie days. The former homicide cop occasionally counsels

At the Pink Pistol

fathers of other celebrities about security and protection from threats and stalkers, things no parent can bear to think about. He worries constantly about Miranda's safety and once hired someone to surreptitiously oversee her bodyguards. She spotted the plant right away. "My Daddy hired you, didn't he?" she snapped. Busted!

The Lambert hospitality knows no bounds. As Bev and Rick began to explain their newest enterprise, a wine company, it was decided that a wine tasting was in order. Although Lindale is advertised as the "blackberry capital" of Texas, Bev says, "I ain't seen a blackberry since I lived here. Ain't nobody growin' no blackberries." Instead, it seems, they are growing grapes. Lambert wines (with labels designed by Luke) are attracting attention with their hilarious names or descriptions, like Crazy Ex-Girlfriend (a "sweet, white, dance-naked-on-the-bar" wine), Kerosene, and Electric Pink, a blush, of course.

An example of the Team Lambert approach to business can be found in one of their wine labels. Miranda positioned her dream car, her candy-apple-red pickup truck, in a field of wildflowers. Bev photographed it and sent the image to Luke, who used it to develop a label for Red 55, a cabernet sauvignon. They enjoy these family pursuits. They work hard, putting in long days on their various enterprises, and are deservedly proud of the many accomplishments.

Since 2003, when Miranda signed with Epic Records, Bev and Rick have been there to see the amazing rise in popularity and acclaim of their beloved, talented daughter. Rick says that seeing his peers and his own musical heroes respecting her music is the most rewarding part. He has written lyrics for her but no longer backs her up on guitar. Bev and Rick travel to events and shows, proud of the hundreds of honors Miranda has earned in a relatively short time. She has won all the big awards: Grammys, *Billboard* Music Awards, truckloads of Country Music Association Awards, and an unheard-of seven consecutive awards for female vocalist of the year from the Academy of Country Music.

She is beloved in the country music industry and usually gets good press. But her recent divorce from Blake Shelton caused a lot of pain for the whole family. Bev found it "excruciating to endure the horrible untruths" that were published. She is infuriated, too, when reports are published about Miranda's weight, whether it's a loss or a gain. "I want to scream, 'IT'S ABOUT THE MUSIC, ASSHOLES!'"

It's also about character and integrity. Bev finds her daughter's kindness and compassion remarkable. She remembers a very early day when Miranda read aloud some album notes from a record they were listening to. She doesn't recall the name of the musician, just that he was thanking his crew, one by one, for their long years of service. Miranda turned to her and said, "That's how I'm going to run my company. I'm going to be so good to them that they will never want to leave me."

As I head out to my car, Bev invites me to peek inside one of the two Airstream trailers parked on the driveway. Rick recently bought it for Bev, and Miranda had it decorated in a tapestry theme in honor of Bev's favorite Carole King album. Family and friends sent her pieces of clothing that were significant in some way, like the shirt Rick wore when he played with Miranda at the Grand Ole Opry. The pieces were patched together into quilts and curtains. Miranda told her, "This is the tapestry of your life."

And like Bev, it is colorful, held together by family pieces. And completely unique.

VIGNETTE #2:

MY FRIEND WENDY

Wendy Cobain O'Connor and I met in 1992 as the tsunami wave of Nirvana's fame was cresting. The secret of the small Seattle band was out. It was in New York City, where a weekend of MTV and *Saturday Night Live* engagements would propel the wave to crash onto airwaves and charts and surprise the world.

This was Wendy's first trip to New York and she was giddy with excitement. We were driven in chauffeured black vans to the backstage doors of the MTV studios and escorted by admiring young staffers to the stage area where the band was preparing for a live performance. I instantly noted that Wendy didn't look much older than the band onstage, her blond bangs and casual skirt and blouse a great disguise for the mother who was about to be forever linked to a musical icon, the "voice of a generation," as some were saying.

We felt an instant connection. Two mothers from unremarkable places with two remarkable sons making groundbreaking music. We bragged a lot, almost competitively. She told me that Kurt had always, as long as she could remember, been writing—on walls, in notebooks. He also drew pictures to illustrate his words. I countered that the musical genius of my son had been apparent shortly after he was out of his playpen. I may have exaggerated. But it was clear that we had both had long musical journeys, and we loved remembering them together.

She said that she and Kurt had always been close, even though family circumstances often separated them. He had wanted her to be in New York that weekend, to share in the excitement of Nirvana's surprising breakthrough, to be in the audience so he could see her. Now, as she remembers that event-filled weekend, she recalls Kurt on the edge of the *Saturday Night Live* stage, looking out, looking lost. "He was looking for me," she said. "He always did that. It made him feel safe . . . because really he was scared."

Celebrating Nirvana's
success with Wendy, 1992

Wendy, my daughter, Lisa, and I went to the hotel bar for drinks that first day while the boys were doing press. We had been swept up in the excitement of our fancy hotel, the energy of the big city, and the royal treatment we were being given. We toasted our sons' success and chatted endlessly about them. There were no sad stories of the past or worries for the future. We were having too much fun. We were in New York! Our boys were successful beyond our wildest dreams. We were excited for them and oh so proud.

The meteoric rise to fame was, we now know, a journey that would too soon end our blissful, innocent joy. The happy memories remain, but as the joy subsided they were replaced by the tragedy, anguish, and incomparable loss of Kurt's suicide in 1994.

When I decided to go on my "meet the mothers" journey, Wendy was uppermost in my mind. She was the first "rock mom" I met. We have stayed in touch over the years, but there have been long gaps, painful times when we had no communication, when tragedy and change pulled us in different directions. There would be a note now and then with a baby picture of Frances, her granddaughter, a few phone calls, a family dinner. And then the Hall of Fame reunion.

I was worried about Wendy coming to the 2014 event that would induct Nirvana into the Rock and Roll Hall of Fame. How could her excruciating loss allow her to enjoy the film clips, the speeches, the cameras, the memories—all compressed into one night? She surprised me. She was brilliant:

strong, beautiful as ever in a dark-blue gown, and touched by the tributes to the son she called her "angel."

The night before the event, the original Nirvana crew gathered at a small midtown bar for a reunion. Wendy and I had some time to talk as we hugged all the "kids" who had worked behind the scenes during the rapid shift when the band grew from playing tiny clubs to headlining in huge arenas. She was excited about a film project she was working on that would tell Kurt's story. She was hopeful, believing that the process she was embarking on would be "therapeutic," as she put it.

Sadly, the documentary to which she devoted so much time and effort yielded no such outcome. It devastated her. She felt betrayed by her portrayal as an uncaring, distant mother. She broke down, and it took a long time for her to recover. After that, how could she go through the process of replaying the past with any trust that the result would match her memories? She couldn't take any more pain.

I understood. All the mothers I talked to had some misgivings. I have had them, too, over the years, refusing to give interviews unless I really trusted the writer. Even so, out of the three interviews I gave, one writer published my home address in his story. You can imagine the resulting cul-de-sac traffic and uninvited guests that caused!

On the most recent anniversary of Kurt's death, I called Wendy to tell her I was thinking about her. We talked for a very long time and decided not to do a typical interview, but Wendy wanted me to share in this book the things I remember about Kurt that comforted her when I recalled them for her, occasions that reminded her of his shy, sweet nature. Will these small snippets of time and place satisfy a reader's thirst for the whole story? I don't know. I wonder if anyone knows the whole story. I have only a few pieces of it, scenes recorded in my mind like faded snapshots in an old scrapbook.

Escaping cameras and fans and industry advisors was a venture that began soon after *Nevermind* was released. Quiet places were rare. Our homes were the only safe zones. My house served as the place of refuge one weekend when Nirvana played in DC. David hosted the band, the crew, and a few close friends at a barbecue there. Some drank beer on the patio or played badminton in the backyard. A small group gathered in my tiny living room, forming a circle for conversation. I vividly recall that Kurt placed himself outside the circle, sitting quietly, slightly separate from the rest. I joined him and we talked about some of the books on the shelves behind us. I gave him my copy of Ray Bradbury's *Dandelion Wine* and urged him to read it. I have always thought it should be staged with music. He promised to read it. I don't remember the rest of our conversation, only that we talked about ideas and books, not the craziness that was surrounding him. I was delighted to listen to the quiet, introspective Kurt, who smiled and conversed easily, still outside the group. That was the Kurt Wendy loves to remember.

Another recollection that amuses her was when I was visiting David in Seattle. Krist and Kurt stopped by for a short visit, and I took a photo of Kurt. He was grinning. That scene still plays in my head: a simple moment when three friends were laughing together, enjoying themselves. It was a rare Seattle moment. Kurt was smiling and the sun was shining.

A last brief glimpse of the young star occurred at the 1991 Reading Festival in England. The cold wind was whipping the tents dangerously, and several days of rain had created acres of mud, upon which stood sixty thousand screaming fans. On that enormous stage Nirvana was thrilling their audience with song after song. Then Kurt stepped to the microphone and announced, "Guess what? Today is Dave's mom's birthday. Let's sing to her!" I was pulled onstage, and all those fans sang "Happy Birthday" to me as I stood dumbfounded but quite delighted at the celebration.

Wendy wants to hold on to moments like that. Sunshine, smiles, and celebrations have been rare commodities in her life. As her friend, I hope that someday she will get her share.

Kurt,
smiling in Seattle

MICHAEL DIAMOND

(MIKE D)

Born: November 20, 1965, in New York, New York

Beastie Boys (1980–2012): Rapping, vocals, drums, percussion, keyboard

Genres: Hip-hop, rap rock, hardcore punk, alternative hip-hop

First Album: *Polly Wog Stew* (1982)

HESTER DIAMOND

Mother of Mike D
(Beastie Boys)

IT IS THE UPPER WEST SIDE of New York City, across the street from Central Park. Carefully coiffed women in furs are escorted to black cars. A few fit-looking young women pass by with tiny, equally well-coifed dogs on leashes. It is not a locale where one would expect a young white rapper, hat askew, arms splayed, to burst from an elegant facade, screaming, "You gotta fight—for your right—to pa-a-ar-ty!"

Michael Diamond did just that. It may seem an unlikely story, but listen closely as his intellectual, somewhat imperious mother tells of their respective journeys through untested, unpredicted territories. Both mother and son made breakthroughs that created profitable careers and international reputations.

Hester Klein was born two months after the Great Stock Market Crash of 1929. The comfortable, middle-class life in the Bronx that her engineer father had provided was disrupted by the economic woes that led to ten years of the Great Depression. Building projects stopped and he lost his job. But her family resumed a bit of normalcy when he became part of the WPA as a teacher of mechanical drawing. Their lives were fairly typical of those of millions of others: careful, frugal, and closely affected by national and international affairs. World War II and the mobilization that preceded it provided jobs and fear in equal measures.

Hester was a bright, curious child. She says, "I had the kind of parents who never told me I was pretty, never told me I was smart." But

41

she recalls having a growing awareness of the fact that she was intelligent. And parents in those days didn't often praise or flatter, so there was no resentment or rebellion.

Curious about Europe and the larger world beyond the Bronx, Hester tried to enlist her maternal grandfather to tell stories of his Latvian roots, but she was rebuffed. He believed assimilation, not looking into the past, was key. His silence, of course, made her more curious and eager to learn, even if she had to do it alone. Years later she continued to reach outside her culture, learning three foreign languages entirely on her own.

World War II was responsible for a major shift in Hester's life, what she calls her "self-taught art education." Her school, Hunter High School, was next to and affiliated with Hunter College, which the US Navy appropriated to use as a training area for the WAVES, the newly created women's division. The high school's schedule was modified so that the students began classes very early in the morning and finished by one o'clock, allowing the classrooms to be used by the WAVES. Hester spent the afternoons touring the city's museums. She became completely enchanted by the Museum of Modern Art. Having never been an artist or art student and knowing nothing at all about modern art, she was drawn in an almost mystical way to the paintings she saw. She stood for hours before "these strange pictures," trying to figure them out. Her curiosity demanded to know: Why did the painter do that? Why is this color here? What's the connection between this picture and that one? Why does the museum have them organized this way? These were rather sophisticated questions for a teenager with no background in art, one who was alone in the city trying to fill her unexpectedly free afternoons in some worthwhile way.

She laughs now when she describes her "execrable" taste in choosing as her favorite picture a large painting by Pavel Tchelitchew, *Hide-and-Seek*. She thought the images of fetuses and babies and the huge dark tree that centered them were quite profound. She gazed at it for hours.

Her parents were unaware of her newfound passion and would have regarded it, she says, as one of the incomprehensible things that set Hester apart. Her young boyfriend, however, asked to join her on her museum outings. The other kids were going to movies and to have ice cream sodas, but the two of them headed to MOMA. "It was just my luck that he was as responsive as I," she says, "because we didn't even have the vocabulary to discuss things. We would stand together and say, 'Look at that.' That was the limit of our articulateness about paintings."

After college, at age twenty-two, Hester married Harold Diamond, her MOMA mate. He became a teacher and she a social worker. They decided to begin collecting art immediately. Their small salaries were carefully budgeted, but the three-hundred-dollar limit they set for art purchases was hard to come by. When they learned that most artists would sell a work on a payment plan of twenty-five dollars a month, Hester said they made deals with artists "all over town."

They discovered their first "genius," a sixty-year-old abstract-geometric artist who was married to an Irish poet. Through her they met interesting, exotic artists and poets, including Dylan Thomas. But the relationship ended when the jealous artist learned that they were also buying from other artists.

Early days, Michael & Hester

Michael, the equestrian

That's how they started. They bought what they loved, never making a selection for investment purposes. "I have never at any point in my life had investment in mind when I bought art," Hester insists. With an unerring eye, Harold bought and collected art for the rest of his life and became one of the foremost art dealers in New York.

The three Diamond children, David, Stephen, and Michael, were raised by their art-dealer parents in an affluent household on the Upper West Side. Hester insisted on certain family priorities. Because much of Harold and Hester's work required dinner meetings and evening events, she crafted a careful regimen. Michael, the youngest, got home from school first, and Hester was on hand each day with milk and cookies and fifteen minutes of conversation about the day. Each child had his own fifteen minutes, all they wanted or needed, she says. Thursday through Sunday the whole family sat down together for dinner. It was important, required.

Hester learned to appreciate the individual personalities of her three boys. "You couldn't design a family with three boys more different from each other," she said. "David was born talking, Stephen was born smiling." And Michael? He was "royal in his inclinations, a real control freak." She described how Michael often found a way to make the entire family wait for him to finish something, to be "slow on purpose" in order to control the situation. But she understood his frustrations. As the youngest, he wanted to be as good at things as his brothers, who were four and seven years older, and that was usually impossible.

The family traveled extensively during the summers. A trip to Italy involved renting a villa near Florence. Every other day there would be an outing to a nearby city. On alternate days, mornings would be spent in Florence before returning to the house for lunch and an afternoon swim. Those were Michael's favorite days. His older brothers were excited by the art and history they were being introduced to, but Michael tired of it early. Still, even after Hester arranged for him to stay home to swim and play soccer with a caretaker, he insisted on trying to keep up with his older brothers. Hester vividly recalls a day in Rome when a tour of churches was on the itinerary. Michael dragged himself to the top steps of the last cathedral, plopped himself down, and loudly announced, "No more churches!"

Years later, though, he let her know that those early art-history lessons had had an effect. While on tour in Rome, he called her for travel advice, asking where to go to look at fountains and sculptures (still no churches), and she happily obliged. Michael buys art now from young, emerging artists. Hester credits him with having "exquisite taste" and the ability to hang art pieces (her "favorite indoor sport") perfectly.

When Michael was ten, he asked permission to stay after school for drum lessons. He requested a drum set for Christmas and began playing every day in his room. (An agreement was reached with the neighbors that there would be no drumming between seven and eight p.m. to accommodate their dinner hour.) For Michael, the music had begun.

Hester was surprised by his interest in music. There were no musicians in the family and no great interest in any kind of music beyond Frank Sinatra. She always thought her son was a good writer, especially with comic writing, and noted that he drew very well. She describes him as "super bright." She and her husband thought "his difficulty was going to be choosing among his many gifts." It never occurred to them that music and performing would be among them. They hadn't heard drumrolls in the distance signaling the importance of this new phase.

Mike attended Saint Ann's, a prestigious private school, and played music with friends there. He also went to shows in small clubs around town, which is how he met his Beastie Boys bandmates, who all went to different schools. They began as a four-piece hardcore band, playing their first gig at member Adam Yauch's seventeenth birthday party in 1981.

In the early '80s new music scenes were emerging in New York. Punk, hip-hop, and rap, all high-energy forces, propelled young artists to create fresh collaborations of written, spoken, recorded, and performed work. There was no rule book, no playbook.

Certainly there was no "Guide for Parents." Hester, whose last interest in music had been "Ol' Blue Eyes," hadn't a clue. But the unflappable mother understood. "My kids each staked out an interest in something we knew nothing about." Perhaps she saw that they were mirroring her adolescent love affair with art, a subject foreign to her own parents.

There were worries, though. The club dates were usually downtown, in areas where drug use and street crime proliferated. Hester urged Michael to take cabs, not the subway, to stay safe. After the band was formed, Michael assured her he'd be OK. "Ma, you don't understand. The Hells Angels are scared of us!"

I am not a music historian or cultural analyst, just an observer, but I don't believe many other bands have exploded into fame the way the Beastie Boys did. Soon after the 1981 birthday party, they made a record, attracted the attention of the very young producer Rick Rubin, began playing the New York club circuit, and opened for Madonna. Hester remarked, "The whole course of [Mike's] life was bizarre. He was a big star at nineteen!"

But he was also expected to go to college. Mike enrolled at Vassar. Hester puts it this way: "I'm not sure he ever showed up, but he certainly didn't open a book." After the first term, the school requested that he take a term off and return in September ready to work. This forced Hester into one of the most difficult decisions she ever had to make as a mother. She demanded that Mike find a job and an apartment. An eighteen-year-old with a high school diploma was not considered a prize in the New York City employment market, but Mike finally found a job as a stock boy in French's bookstore because he was the only applicant who could alphabetize. He found an apartment as well.

The first time Hester saw the Beastie Boys perform was at a show in Alphabet City. Before that, she'd only seen Michael perform once, when he was in sixth grade, in a production of *Jesus Christ Superstar*. In it he played the drums onstage and "was very joyful doing it," she recalls. Hester headed to the downtown venue, an old dance hall with an open floor downstairs and a second-floor balcony with seating. Michael had suggested she sit there, and Hester soon understood why. When the music started, the floor below became a mosh pit, a tornadic mass of young, fearless lovers of chaos. From her safe perch Hester was astonished to see the bodysurfing and immediately realized "how crazy it was going to be." She would have to rethink an earlier comment she had made when Michael told her he was going to make music his career. "I, ever supportive," she recalls sardonically, "said that's just an excuse for not working."

After this initiation, Hester became an unlikely fan of her son's band. "Rock and roll was a total mystery to me. I don't understand music. But I loved going to their concerts. To me they weren't about music, but about energy and unbelievable rapport with the audience." She is, after all, a woman who understands sudden, surprising connections to art. Before she left the show, a young fan ran to embrace her and thank her for bringing Mike D into the world.

Hester remembers a particular Madison Square Garden performance. She was seated early so she could take it all in. As the opening band played, she observed the audience, restless, milling about, some moving with "a kind of ghetto strut." As she looked around to make note of where the exits were, "in case it got nasty," the Beastie Boys jumped into the light "and fifteen thousand people began screaming when my kid ran out onstage!"

I asked Hester to compare Michael's love of music with her love of art. Both seemed to be powerful forces that mystically took hold and surprised. She said, "I've never been very self-conscious about some things. My love for art was so natural and so powerful that it just felt like breathing. So when Michael was that way about music, I didn't even question it."

During this time Michael kept in close touch with Hester and the family, allowing her opportunities to congratulate him on his progress. "I never expected my kids to confide in me," she said. "We weren't that kind of family. But we were close, sure of each other's love."

Reviewing the Beastie Boys' long career reveals an interesting evolution. The boys were only fifteen when they formed the band and nineteen when their debut album, *Licensed to Ill,* sold fifty million copies worldwide. Their early tours featured controversial hijinks as the press focused on their outrageous behaviors. In LA, they threw chairs from the windows of the Sunset Marquis Hotel into the pool below. They cut a hole in the floor of a Holiday Inn. They were banned from certain hotels and from the CBS headquarters for troublesome incidents. They were at risk for being better known for their antagonistic behavior than for their music. Yet eventually sanity was restored. As they matured they regained perspective, which included broadening the scope of their subject matter from their early "party hard" themes to serious societal issues. By 1999 they were known for the series of Tibetan Freedom Concerts they organized and for taking stands against discrimination and sexual assault. In 2012, a year after their eighth studio album was released, they were inducted into the Rock and Roll Hall

Virginia &
Hester

Beastie Boys'
awards

of Fame. A year later member Adam Yauch died of cancer, and the band was finished.

During the time when the shenanigans of the Beastie Boys turned up the volume of publicity, Hester turned her attentions to her own brave new venture, the Medici Archive Project. As a founder and president, she was responsible for funding, through grants and donations, a program that is making a major contribution to the scholarship of the Medici Archives. Culling through over six thousand volumes of records dated from 1537 to 1743, the new archivists have brought to modern technology the most comprehensive record of every aspect of life in early-modern Europe that exists today. The project makes available long-hidden information on political, diplomatic, gastronomic, economic, artistic, scientific, military, and medical cultures of that time. It is a mighty contribution.

Hester is proud of that accomplishment but was willing to hand it over when she felt it was time to move on. Her most recent project is VISTAS (Visual Images of Sculpture in Time and Space), a nonprofit organization that publishes scholarly books on sculpture. She has plans to accompany Michael and his family on a safari in Botswana. That trip will round out another busy year for Hester Diamond.

As I take my last glances around Hester's magnificent penthouse apartment overlooking Central Park, at the royal-blue sculpted chair, the bright fuchsia print on the couches, and the crayon-box colors on the rug, she stops to tell me about her latest thing. She has invented a new walker, one that will be practically and aesthetically superior to the one she reaches for now. It will be on the market very soon. I hope it has a fifth gear!

GARY LEE CLARK JR.

Born: February 15, 1984, in Austin, Texas

Gary Clark Jr. (1996–present): Vocals, guitar, drums, trumpet, keyboard

Genres: Blues, rock, soul

First Album: *110* (2004)

SANDI CLARK

Mother of
Gary Clark Jr.

GARY CLARK JR. HAS BEEN CALLED "The Chosen One," "the new Hendrix," "a living legend at thirty-one," and proclaimed by President Obama to be "the future." He's a musician's musician, the go-to guy to fill a roster of elites. In the past year he has played blues, jazz, or rock with Paul McCartney, Beyoncé, B.B. King, Joe Walsh, Mick Jagger, and Buddy Guy, to name just a few.

Sandi and Gary Clark Sr. have been in the audience for most of those performances, often watching in disbelief that their shy, handsome son has made it to this level. They have always believed in him, supported him, but this rarefied air forces a gasp or two. After all, it seems not that long ago that they had to drive him to the clubs where he was playing three years before he was eligible for a driver's license. And because liquor was served in those places, one of the parents had to stay with him for the duration of his playing time.

"My husband and I used to tag team," Sandi explained. When Gary was thirteen or fourteen he had a once-a-week gig at Jazz, an Austin restaurant that he outlasted, for an early happy-hour set. Sandi, just home from work, took him to the club and sat on a bench with her eight-year-old daughter, who would put her head on Sandi's lap and nap. When her husband got off work, he took the rest of the shift so she could take Savannah home and start dinner for the family of six.

He was so young! Sandi thought so, too. "I remember when he turned fourteen, they announced at Joe's Generic Bar that he was now 'the *fourteen*-year-old Gary Clark Jr.,' and I thought fourteen sounded so much older than thirteen!"

It was also hard to grasp that the young teen had been given his first guitar only two years earlier, when he was twelve.

Sometimes Sandi felt guilty and conflicted. "What am I doing here with my kid who should be home?" She had to constantly remind herself that this was what he so passionately wanted to do—even though her mother's instinct thought he should be doing his homework and getting ready for bed. This was vastly different from her own childhood.

Sandi's upbringing had been strictly conservative. Her father was a staff sergeant in the Air Force who raised his five children on a military income on Air Force bases in California, Florida, Michigan, and Guam. His authority was not questioned, but Sandi describes him as a "phenomenal man," fiercely devoted to his family. Like most military kids she and her sisters and brothers adjusted easily to changing addresses and new adventures. Until the last one. Sandi was enjoying her high school friends and activities in Guam, where she was popular, a cheerleader. But at the end of her junior year the family moved to Austin, Texas, where she would have to spend her senior year in a new city and try to make new friends during the year when most of her classmates were celebrating their old ones.

That was the toughest move, but the already close sisters held together, which they continue to do to this day. All are still in Austin and are a part of each others' families.

Sandi's father was proud when she earned a scholarship to the University of Texas, but he refused to allow her to live on campus. She had to take buses back and forth from their home in Austin and call her mother to pick her up when computer lab sessions lasted till midnight. Without begging, arguing, or stomping her feet, Sandi made her first defiant move. She signed all the paperwork necessary to get a dorm room and prepared to move in.

Upon learning of this mutinous act, her father "marched me to the head of housing on the UT campus and said, 'My daughter is NOT going to live on campus.'" The college official shrugged it off. "She's of legal age to sign a contract. You two need to work it out."

And they did. As they walked away, her father acknowledged that this was something she felt she must do and had figured out for herself.

Sandi the cheerleader

Perhaps he was pleased with her newly found self-assurance. Certainly he was aware that his child was becoming an adult.

Sandi, a self-described nerd, spent all her time studying, never missing a class or lab. Her friends, though, insisted that she leave her room just once. They went to her closet, picked out some clothes, and pulled her out the door to go to a campus party. It was there that she met Gary Clark. And that was that. Both were twenty-four when they married in 1981.

Their first child was born a year after they married, and three more followed. Their life together, defined by parenthood, was not always easy, but Sandi and Gary focused on creating a strong family ethic. Grandparents, aunts, uncles, and cousins broadened those ties. It was a stable marriage. As in all such unions, there were some tough times, Sandi recalls, "But I always knew I didn't want my son to be another young black man without a father figure. That was always in my mind. I didn't want to give Gary an excuse to not live up to his potential. So we always focused on that. We didn't want the whole dad-on-weekends sort of thing."

Sandi describes Gary Jr. as a "pretty easy" child, always respectful, with lots of friends and typical interests. Until, of course, he got his first guitar at age twelve. Gary Jr.'s story is that he had wanted a guitar "forever." But Sandi thinks "forever" was just a year. She and her husband bought one for him as a Christmas gift. As is true of any musical instrument he touches, his proud mother says, he was almost instantly proficient. His father often sat on the stairs outside Gary Jr.'s room listening to the new sounds coming from behind the closed door, shaking his head. "He's really good, Sandi!" he said.

They weren't prepared for that much-too-early, self-taught prowess. How could they have been? Sandi has a distant memory of taking her son to a Jackson 5 show when he was four years old. Gary Jr. now says that was the first moment he knew he wanted to perform on a stage. But it wasn't Michael he was drawn to; it was Tito and his guitar.

Once Gary Jr. had his own guitar, his connection to the instrument and to the music he so adeptly drew from it became his unquestioned priority. He played music with friends and began showing up at jazz clubs for blues jams, weeknight events where there were sign-up sheets and the musicians were assigned to play with others who had also signed up. There was no way to predict what might happen, but Sandi remembers some surprisingly good music resulting from those musical lotteries. Sadly, most of those small jazz clubs are gone now. Even in Austin, where music is a major force and the city motto is "Keep Austin Weird," jazz is a fading genre.

I recently read that Gary had admitted to an interviewer that he played without a set list, so when I had a chance to talk to him I asked if that was a residual effect of those early jazz-club days. His answer showed how much things have changed in the past few years: "That used to be my thing because I thought I could get away with being wild and free, being in the moment. But then I realized it was kinda selfish and irresponsible seeing as how now I've got a crew of people wondering what's going on. When we first started playing gigs we wouldn't have a set list because we didn't have a set band. We had different rotating rhythm sections every night. We would play familiar blues songs and maybe a song I had written in folky, smoky blues bars where in between songs people were joking and laughing, beers dropping and glass breaking or whatever. People were entertaining themselves. It wasn't like a show."

As Gary Jr.'s musical proficiency increased, his interest in school declined. His grades plummeted. Sandi and Gary Sr., after asking Sandi's mother for advice, took Gary Jr.'s guitar away, promising to hand it back over when his grades improved. Soon thereafter, Sandi says, "I watched the energy drain from him. He got dark circles under his eyes. He had no personality. And his grades didn't improve." Unwilling to further her son's misery, Sandi gave the guitar back to him and hoped for the best. "In retrospect, I get it," she says. "He had a vision early about where he was headed in his life. My husband and I supported him on his journey, but we knew the odds weren't in his favor. Not because we doubted his talent, but because it's such a competitive business and more people struggle to make it than actually do. So education was important to me. I wanted good grades and the college degree. But he wasn't having it. I was always taking the car away or grounding him. Nothing worked."

Gary wanted to make them happy, so he struggled on in school, turning in projects late, repeating classes, trying to catch up. He recalls being headstrong, determined to convince his mother that being in school wasn't worth his time. "She didn't see my vision," he says. "'You just don't get it, Mom. You don't get it! I want to be a successful musician!'"

Gary wanted to be playing or listening to music 24/7. When he was sixteen he earned the nickname "Hotwire" by climbing out his second-story bedroom window to a porch roof, carefully sidling to the edge where he would give the family dog a treat to keep him from barking, hopping to the fence below, and hot-wiring the family car. He went to clubs to listen to music, occasionally getting called to the stage. Sometimes he just drove around Austin listening to music on the radio, letting it fill the car and his head. He couldn't get enough.

Payback came when Gary Sr. discovered one night that his car and his son were missing. The open bedroom window was the only clue the parents needed. Sandi crawled into Gary Jr.'s bed, pulled up the covers, and waited for him to return through the window. (Now Hotwire is the name of Gary Clark Jr.'s record label.)

By the time he graduated from high school, Gary knew many of the blues and jazz musicians on the Austin scene. He had played in most of the clubs and earned a reputation as one to watch. But no one knew where to go next. Sandi, recently laid off from her job as an accountant, wanted to help. "I really believed in him," she said. She bought Donald Passman's book *All You Need to Know About the Music Business,* studied it, and learned how to make CDs and put together press kits. She agreed to finance Gary's first foray into the great unknown and to help him get his music out. She created a website for him, putting snippets of his newest music on it along with ordering information. When she and Gary loaded their van with boxes of the newly pressed CDs, she remembers how proud and happy he was. "He just wanted to drop them from a plane so everyone could hear them!"

The manager/accountant/mom who was booking shows for him thought that selling the CDs from the website and at shows was a better idea. She insisted on keeping inventory. The first time Gary sold ninety-nine CDs at a show, when he was eighteen, he thanked her profusely, recognizing the value of her determination to run his affairs profes-

Grandma's house

With Sandi applauding our sons at a 4th of July show

sionally. Sandi stepped away from her position as manager when it was clear that Gary needed an experienced pro to help his career along. But she remains his accountant, responsible for the payroll, for paying his bills, and for maintaining his books.

Yet—and I found this astounding—Sandi steps back from any acknowledgement of her contributions. She doesn't feel comfortable with a VIP sticker slapped on her jacket, doesn't feel she has the right to go backstage, where her son and the superstars he is playing with are gathered. Like her son she is very shy and unassuming and humble. "I just don't feel deserving," she says. Sandi recognizes that same modesty in her son. When I asked her what she thought set him apart, she said, "He's just so humble. He can't figure out what the big deal is, why everybody thinks he's so good." She adds, however, that the shyness disappears "when you put a guitar in his hand. Then he's a different person."

The past ten years have yielded many accolades and honors for Gary Clark Jr. In addition to winning several Austin music awards (and having the mayor proclaim a Gary Clark Jr. Day when he was only seventeen), he has made lists of "Bests" in *Spin* and *Rolling Stone,* and in 2014 he won a Grammy and the Blues Foundation's Contemporary Blues Male Artist of the Year award.

His mom and dad are thrilled by the major venues where their son now plays. They traveled to London to see a memorable show at the Royal Albert Hall, where he played with Eric Clapton. Another was a Madison Square Garden show. In that enormous arena, sold out and throbbing with the energy of thousands of expectant fans, a single light beamed onto a lone man with his guitar. Seeing her son spotlighted in that huge arena "brought tears to my eyes," Sandi says.

One of Gary Clark Jr.'s greatest shows was played in one of the smallest rooms, the East Room of the White House, in a notable 2012 tribute to American blues music. Gary remembers the day twenty years earlier when the Clark family stood outside the White House gates as President Bill Clinton's motorcade rolled through. His sister was certain that the President's wave was directed specifically to her while Gary was wondering what it was like inside those gates. He would find out. The night of the 2012 show, he talked with President Obama about music and played with his idols Buddy Guy, B.B. King, Mick Jagger, and Jeff Beck in a magnificent hour topped off by the President picking up the mic and joining the stellar crew in "Sweet Home Chicago." Gary says the evening flashed by, "but when I think about it now I'm like, man, I can't believe that really happened!"

In 2014 Gary Jr. and Nicole Trunfio became engaged and the following year had a son, Zion. In 2016 they married at Coachella, the place where they had met. Although other grandparents are downsizing, enjoying their empty nests, the Clarks still love gathering their large, expanding clan around them. A plaque on Sandi's front door announces, "What happens at Grandma's stays at Grandma's." Loosely translated, it means pillow fights and sugar treats will be allowed and secrets will be safely kept—a surprising turn from a mom at one time nicknamed "Sarge" by her son's friends. Sandi first learned of that moniker a few months ago when a friend of Gary's let it slip. She told Gary that it hurt her feelings to think that his friends remembered her as being mean. Her son assured her that the name referred only to the strict discipline she imposed, and he said he intended to carry on that tradition with his own son. She's very happy to hear that validation. "We had rules and curfew, but I think those things matter."

They might matter even more in our sons' privileged households. A grandmotherly discussion followed about the perils we never had to address but that we see in the future for our successful kids. They will face challenges and choices we were spared because of our limited finances. They will struggle to keep their own children from feeling entitled and being spoiled. They will need to balance the wonders of financial security with the need for compassion and understanding toward those who don't share it. Their values will have to be strong and clearly asserted. It won't be easy.

Meeting and getting to know Sandi Clark was like participating in a senior version of Mommy and Me, the program that brings together first-time mothers and their newborns to discuss issues faced by new parents. It turns out that grandparents, too, are comforted by knowing there are others with the same concerns. It's refreshing to talk openly about them.

Perhaps Sandi and I can feel less guilty about the fact that we still find things to worry about. After all, our sons have established themselves in the music business. They are respected and loved by their peers and their fans. They are financially secure and have settled into family life. They have bright futures. Nevertheless, a mother is a mother. When Gary is on a tour and Sandi knows they're headed to snowy areas, she will ask, "Are you guys paying attention to the weather?" and encourage him to throw an extra coat into his suitcase. Sometimes, when he looks tired, she'll remind him to take care of himself. Usually an "I know, Mama" with a hug is the response she gets. And then he's off again.

Gary's calendar is filled with festivals, special events, small clubs, huge arenas, and every now and then a TV appearance—and "he's still the same kind, gentle soul he's always been," Sandi says. She offered proof of this by telling me of a midnight call from Gary to his father: "I get it, Dad. I get what you've been doing all these years, trying to take care of Mom and the family for as long as I can remember. I get you, Dad. Thank you. I love you for it."

Sandi keeps scrapbooks in the hopes that Gary Jr. will look back on their pages someday and recall the early times and places in his career. "Not how many tickets he was selling or how much he was being paid for a show, but what his fans were seeing and hearing and writing about. I want him to remember that he really moved people." The title of her scrapbook should probably be what she and her son say often: it's all about the music.

VIGNETTE #3

THE MUSIC LADY

Her name was Alice Louise but everyone called her Toots. She was my mother's half sister and her complete opposite. Tall, close to six feet, with long Olive Oyl legs that were surprisingly athletically adept, she was loud, demonstrative, a great lover of friends, parties, dances, life! She had no children so I was the beneficiary of much of the exuberant love and fun she radiated. We went on spur-of-the-moment road trips in her little Dodge convertible with a rumble seat: lakeside beach days, picnics in Youngstown, Ohio's beautiful Mill Creek Park. She was one of the first women to sign up for the WAVES during World War II and wore the crisp white uniform and dapper hat with great pride. I adored her.

When Toots was suffering the final, grotesque stages of Alzheimer's disease, I visited her at the residential nursing hospital, which was populated by others in various stages of that plague. She brightened a bit as I entered her room, but she didn't know who I was. Her mother? Her sister? Her friend? She knew she loved me, though, and smiled as I hugged her. When she tried to leave her bed to go to her bathroom, which was located about four feet away, she had to be redirected. Such was the state of a formerly vibrant mind. I couldn't bear it.

And then there was a tap at the door and the announcement that the "music lady" was downstairs and ready to begin. Toots loved to sing. Her powerful contralto, undecorated by vibrato and untouched by instruction, was loud, perfectly pitched, and rich in tone. When she worked in a bank, her voice often echoed through the two-story marble lobby, inviting the bank's customers to tap their feet in rhythm as they stood in line.

Hand in hand, Toots and I went to the music room and waited for the music lady to begin. Soon we were back in the 1940s. After a short piano introduction the leader sang, "Don't sit under the apple tree with anyone else but me." Then she swept her arm toward Toots and nodded. Toots finished the song, every word, every note perfect. The melody that had been locked in her head unlocked, as all the other things could not. My name could not. Her name could not. But the music could.

Perhaps you've seen documentaries about music and the brain—stories of overnight talent surges, or sudden, unexplained passion for an arcane instrument after a surgery, or therapeutic results from drumming. Learned scholars have presented these cases convincingly.

The music lady, though, had the best tricks. When she reached into the memories of her silenced audience and pulled out song after song, I knew I was witness to a special moment. It was the very essence of music: part magic, pure power.

VIGNETTE #4

THE THREE BELLES

When I was eight years old the world transformed. The 1945 ending of World War II allowed my father Charles (Chirk) Hanlon to complete his service as a Seabee in Iwo Jima and Japan and return to his family. He and my mother, Violet, bought an old farmhouse on six acres of land in a suburb of Youngstown, Ohio, a purchase made possible by the GI Bill.

Most of my memories of childhood and growing up took place on the grassy acres of lawn, the shady front porch, or the small kitchen with a Formica table, that central point of our very modest house. My brother was born there and a few years later my mother became a victim of the polio epidemic of 1949, confined to an iron lung before making a full recovery. A pink sign on our front door announced that we had been quarantined. Yet for the most part those years were unremarkable, arranged around work, family, and school. We were wholesome, my friends and I say. Apathetic, some historians label us. Conformist, silent, docile.

Most of us didn't yet have television to frighten us with Red Scares and the geopolitical changes that were reshaping Europe after the war. We felt secure in our comfortable suburban societies. Our parents did not discuss elections or wars in Asia. They played golf and bridge and once a year danced to Guy Lombardo at the Idora Park Ballroom. They lived to put the Depression and the horrendous wartime behind them.

Discrimination against other races and nationalities and against women abounded, but we didn't take notice. I look back on some situations that would have me screaming "Foul!" now and wish I had used a louder voice. But I hadn't found it yet.

The voice I had found was a clear, perfectly pitched mezzo-soprano. It fit seamlessly between the high soprano of my new friend Sherry and the sultry alto of Jeralyn, one of my oldest friends. Our first performance was for one of the many musical revues Miss Etheleda Szalma, our energetic choir director, put on each year at Boardman High School. She created lavish stage productions that were performed for the school and commu-

The Three Belles,
Ginny, Sherry & Jeralyn

nity, selling out the large auditorium for three-night runs. A most vivid recollection is a *Boardman on Broadway* show in which I sang "I'm Gonna
Wash That Man Right Outa My Hair," from the musical *South Pacific.* For
authenticity, shampoo was provided—Halo, I believe. Unfortunately, that
prop wasn't there for the dress rehearsal, so it was a great (and painful) surprise when on opening night the onstage hair washing yielded no
lather and a whole lot of soap in my eyes. On the second night, however,
my credibility was restored, thanks to the generous application of foamy
shaving cream while I belted out my solo.

For one of her revues Miss Szalma chose Sherry, Jeralyn, and me to
sing "Tea for Two" as a trio. We added a few of our own touches and a bit
of subtle choreography. We realized that we had something very special,
a perfect blend. It surprised us at first, and as we rehearsed we were con-
scious of maintaining it. Turns out we were a big hit!

After that we named ourselves the Three Belles and spent every available minute together building a repertoire from pop music and old standards. It was great fun. Soon requests were coming from Kiwanis clubs,
Lions Clubs, Women's City Clubs, and church groups asking us to perform at local events. Our mothers sewed kelly-green jumpers for us and

surprised us by supporting the occasional performance that required our getting out of school. We were especially thrilled to be invited to sing on a morning cooking show, one of the first local television shows in the Youngstown area. After singing "Alexander's Ragtime Band," "Bewitched, Bothered and Bewildered," and "Easter Parade," we were asked to assist in a local dairy commercial by drinking a glass of milk, creating the most challenging moment of my short singing career. I despise milk.

Life in the Midwest in the mid-1950s revolved around school. The Boardman Stadium was packed for every Friday football game, and there were sock hops after each one. In my bright orange circle skirt and saddle shoes I jitterbugged to Elvis, Fats Domino, and Buddy Holly. Then we slow danced to Nat King Cole, Frank Sinatra, or the Platters. Occasionally the Three Belles would be asked to sing a song or two. A perfect Friday night would end with an invitation by a cute boy in a letter jacket to hop into his shiny two-toned Chevy and head to Swensons, where hamburgers and shakes were delivered to the cars on trays. We did our best to enjoy them before our curfews signaled an end to the evening.

I began arranging music for the trio, although at the time I didn't know that was the term for what I was doing. I was determining harmonies and repetitions and sprinkling in solo parts for Sherry and Jeralyn. I also began writing songs but was very shy about developing my own music for

Reunion,
Ginny, Sherry & Jeralyn

performances. One of my songs, though, "Never Like This," was a favorite with many of our friends.

This was where the music began for me. The vocal trio that was compared to the McGuire Sisters (we thought we were better!) was a central part of my high school years. Yet there was never a thought that we would continue after that. We went to universities in three different states and made our ways in the world in very different ways.

Still, I had to have more music. At Ohio Wesleyan University I sang in musicals and in the women's chorus. I became the Tri-Delts' song leader and continued to write and arrange music for my new, less-promising group. My friend Al Johnson asked me to help him produce traveling skits for campus elections, and he and I created short musical entertainments to be performed at fraternity houses. We wrote *Saturday Night Live*–worthy satirical sketches and parodies that put us in great demand. I almost flunked out of school, but I loved every minute of my time writing and performing.

When I was blessed with my two beautiful children, I had a new trio. I set aside "Twinkle, Twinkle, Little Star" in favor of my own adaptations of the music of the '60s. My poor children were deprived of the classic lullabies, but they loved "You're my Cinderella, you're my Rockefella, ooohhhwee" instead.

The Three Belles recently met in Chicago for a very special, long-awaited reunion. We didn't sing, but we laughed at many memories. Sherry and I chided Jeralyn for our only disastrous performance. It occurred when she dissolved in a fit of uncontrollable giggling at a snooty women's university club. After trying to gracefully wait it out, Sherry and I continued as a duet, and our stricken friend ran off the stage to collapse in a heap of hysteria. She still has no idea what triggered her outburst.

We're all seventy-eight now, and we just don't know what to think of that. Sherry, who has played golf every week of her life, continues to win tournaments. Jeralyn, only recently retired as a theater director, is ready to "unretire." And I am in Chicago for the Foo Fighters' Wrigley Field show, one of the several dozen I've attended this year.

Our paths have diverged but the bond remains strong. The harmony is still a perfect blend.

ESTE ARIELLE,

Born March 14, 1986

DANIELLE SARI,

Born February 16, 1989

& ALANA MYCHAL HAIM

Born December 15, 1991

San Fernando Valley (Los Angeles, California)

HAIM (2007–present): Vocals, guitar, bass, drums, keyboard, percussion

Valli Girls (2005–2007)

Genre: Pop rock

First EP: *Forever* (2012)

First Studio Album: *Days Are Gone* (2013)

DONNA HAIM

Mother of Este, Danielle, and Alana Haim
(HAIM)

A MOTHER SAYS MANY GOOD-BYES. From the first preschool parting—the tiny hand clutching yours, the tenuous steps toward the school door, where you are hoping he will be a "big brave boy" so you can retreat to your car and dissolve in great sobbing gasps of loss—to the first time you hand your car keys to a sixteen-year-old who may or may not be a maniac. These are moments that test the best of us. Many mothers watch their children, tall and straight, somber, crisply uniformed, go off to war—or move across the country or across the world to take a job in a strange place. And, of course, there are the women who say nervous good-byes to fledgling musicians who can't wait to get "on the road again" as Mrs. Nelson's son put it.

We cry a little. We worry a lot. But life goes on. We get back to it. We call our other children and arrange to cook Sunday dinner for them. We babysit for them on Saturday nights and join them at school plays or Little League games. We'll be a phone call away.

Unless, of course, all three go at once. All three beautiful young women! What happens when the family nest empties out into a tour bus?

To hear that story, I called Donna Haim, whose three daughters comprise the rock group HAIM, one of 2015's Grammy nominees for Best New Artist. She lives in "the Valley," only a mile or so from my house, so I invited her over for lunch.

Donna Haim, a vibrant, cheerful woman, works as a real estate agent in the San Fernando Valley area of Los Angeles. Her story begins, though, in Philadelphia, where she grew up. Donna describes her early self as "the assistant to my mother." She was the first child, expected to help with her two younger sisters and one brother. Her mother was very young, fun loving, and gifted with a beautiful voice. She sang on radio shows, but more often danced around the house with her happy brood. Donna grew up with Sinatra and Tony Bennett crooning the classic songs of the 1940s and '50s on the radio while she and her mother sang along. She started dancing lessons at three and piano lessons at seven. But the life change came when her mother arranged for her to take guitar lessons and her teacher bought her her first guitar, a nylon-string Yamaha that cost thirty dollars.

Donna loved her lessons. Unable to put the guitar down, she stayed in her room for hours, writing down words to the songs on the radio and figuring out chords. "I found my voice," she says. Her teacher died very young of multiple sclerosis, but he had given her a foundation and a lifelong passion. Many years later she would pass those gifts on to her own girls.

In high school, as president of the Folk Guitar Club, Donna planned concerts and played in the coffeehouses that were becoming a part of Philadelphia's music scene. The historic city was already home to many genres of music, proud of the world-renowned Philadelphia Orchestra and of Dick Clark's *American Bandstand*. Chubby Checker and Frankie Avalon were hometown favorites topping the rock and pop charts, and a strong current of R&B and jazz flowed through the city. Dozens of venues brought in the best artists of the day. Music was never far away in Philadelphia. Donna couldn't afford tickets to most of the concerts, but a neighborhood friend treated her to some of the best shows in town. Her first concert featured Elton John and James Taylor. She saw the Allman Brothers, David Bowie, and Bonnie Raitt, whose music she continues to idolize.

Do you remember being fifteen? For many women that's about the time we begin to wonder about people and places outside the confines of our regulated lives. We wonder who we are and where we belong. It was at this impressionable age that Donna was invited to visit her aunt in Los Angeles. She saw a new world as she stargazed and went shopping on the Sunset Strip. The little East Coast girl who arrived in California in a pastel dress, knee socks, and pumps returned home in a leather vest, a floppy hat, and moccasins, her guitar slung over her shoulder.

She returned to playing at the Philly coffeehouses and was surprised one night to see her parents in the audience. Undeterred by her warnings that half the audience would be stoned, they sat quietly in a corner, their eyes fixed on the stage. They had both worked all day and had three other children at home to care for, but there they were to support her—on that night and others. Donna never forgot that devotion.

Donna's plan had always been to go to college to prepare to be a teacher. She had volunteered in the reading lab at her old elementary school and knew that she belonged in a profession that would make use of her nurturing nature and love of children. She also dreamed of a home and a family of her own. A meager budget dictated that she would live at home and attend Penn State's Ogontz campus, which was five minutes away, so she enrolled there. After Donna finished a year at Penn State, her father announced that the family was going to move to LA. They left the wonderful house that backed up to a park, the neighbors who were like an extended family, and piled into their old Cadillac for the cross-country drive. Donna was excited to enroll at UCLA and to return to Bel Air, where her aunt lived. She'd be back on the Sunset Strip in no time!

But it didn't work out that way. Donna and her mother tried to mask their disappointment when their new LA home turned out to be far from the Hollywood Hills, in Whittier, close to where her aunt had just moved. To make matters worse, promised renovations to the house had not been done. The kitchen was in shambles. For two months the family cooked outside and worked on the renovations themselves. Their ever-optimistic mother began looking for another house immediately, and after a difficult two years they finally settled into a much better Westside Los Angeles neighborhood, in a house that the family worked hard to make their own. They added hardwood floors, Mexican tiles, and her mother's personal touches. Finally! They were home in LA.

Donna majored in art education at UCLA, and she found friends who loved music as much as she did. They entertained themselves with their guitars, harmonizing vocally as they played the latest pop and folk music. One night they decided to pop in at the Palomino Club, an erstwhile Valley venue that hosted an open-mic night every Monday. Donna's friends encouraged her to take the mic and "do her Bonnie Raitt thing."

Donna's adoration for the sultry-voiced, redheaded guitar maestro had begun when a cousin who loved old Chicago blues music gave her an early Bonnie Raitt album. After that she made it a point to see all Raitt's shows in and around Philadelphia. "I had never heard a woman sing and play the guitar with such passion," Donna said reverently.

She knew all Raitt's songs but particularly liked the bawdy "Let Me Be Your Blender" for the subtle double entendre of its lyrics. It was always a show stopper. That's what she would play for the Palomino open-mic night. No one had any idea there was a talent scout in the audience, a fellow from that year's television sensation, *The Gong Show*. He approached Donna and invited her to be on his program.

Of course she wasn't interested in gracing the stage of a show that was less about talent and more about public humiliation by the dreaded gong. "I'm a serious artist," she snapped at him. "Why would I do that?"

"Well, if you win, you could make some money"—tempting words to an almost-broke student whose "serious artist" persona would not prevail in the brief internal debate that ensued.

Donna took her guitar to the Hollywood Boulevard address the scout gave her, played for two different groups of people, and was told she was in. The second audition was to be held at the NBC studios in Burbank, where hundreds of hopeful dancers, singers, and performers sat in circles chatting nervously or paced the floor warming up. Donna marched in, guitar in one hand, case of hot curlers in the other, ready for the all-day taping session.

She didn't get gonged (hallelujah!). She lost to a father-son act, but six months later she was invited back. This time she agreed instantly. A second appearance would make her eligible for membership in the American Fellowship of Television and Radio Artists. It was worth the try—and she won! "I think the prize was a thousand dollars, which at the time seemed like a million," she recalls. Memories of her nervous walk to the microphone, her introduction by Chuck Barris, and the hundreds of congratulatory phone calls she received from old Philly friends are still strong. The brief moment in the spotlight and the temporary security afforded by her prize money were a nice break in her routine. But this would not be a life changer. Donna got right back to teaching and working in an art gallery. She had rent to pay.

Donna and Mordechai (Moti) Haim met through mutual friends. He was a twenty-seven-year-old Israeli who had come to the United States to play professional soccer in Cleveland, Ohio. It was an exciting prospect, but he arrived from his desert home in the dead of winter, landing in the frozen Midwest. He soon fled farther west to the desert climes of California. He was preparing to return to Israel when they met.

They connected through their love of music. Moti was a drummer and vocalist whose conscription in the Israeli Army had been served in the army band. During the 1973 war the musicians were sent to the front lines to sing and play inspirational songs for the troops to keep their morale up. After Donna and Moti married, they traveled to Israel, where his close-knit family welcomed Donna and she fell in love with the place and the people. But after a year it was time to return to California to begin building their own family.

The Haim girls grew up in a home filled with music of all kinds: the pop and folk tunes of Donna's youth, Latin percussive sounds that their drummer dad loved, and the most current LA radio play. Each girl began piano lessons at three or four, and the three sang together all the time, in the car with their parents and at home with Donna's guitar accompaniment. Donna and Moti enlisted the girls in a family band to play at charity and neighborhood events. Their five-member group, called Rockinhaim, played cover songs from the '50s, '60s, and '70s. Moti was on drums, and Donna and the girls sang and played guitars.

The girls were fortunate to be enrolled in a public school with an outstanding music program. Dixie Canyon Elementary School promised every child a part in a play or musical each year. The woman who taught choir on a volunteer basis put the students onstage for holiday concerts and celebrations throughout the year. George Wyle, who wrote the *Gilligan's Island* theme song, accompanied the students on piano. Each of the Haim girls was enriched by those early performance opportunities, and Donna is grateful for the experiences, which, sadly, most children miss out on.

Este, now six feet tall, sprouted early. She looked older than the classmates she towered over. Her comedic skills began to blossom. She got the lead in a major school play when she was only in second grade

The Haim family

Rockinhaim

and continued to get starring roles throughout her elementary years. Donna predicted that Este would be on *Saturday Night Live* someday and allowed her to stay up late to watch the show, delighting in Este's imitations of the comedians. Roseanne Roseannadanna was a favorite.

After Dixie Canyon, each girl was accepted into the performing-arts magnet program at Millikan Middle School, a public school in the Valley, and at Los Angeles County High School for the Arts, another public performing-arts magnet school. Competition for admission into LACHSA is daunting. Auditions are open to all of the approximately seven hundred thousand students in the nation's second-largest school system for 130 spots per year, only 25 in each specific magnet. The school is highly rated for academic excellence as well as conservatory training in the arts. "Fame High," the nickname given to it by a 2012 award-winning documentary, can brag about the Haim sisters, Taran Killam of *Saturday Night Live* fame, and Josh Groban as famous alumni.

Este majored in drama at LACHSA and won a Shakespeare award when she was in tenth grade. Alana and Danielle majored in opera. All

Doing her Bonnie Raitt thing

thrived and were challenged academically and artistically. Donna had to step up to the challenge as well. School hours were from eight a.m. to four p.m., and the drive from the Haims' home in the Valley to the campus in East LA was a daily trial. Sometimes they took a bus or train part of the way, but the days were always long. The girls all had jobs, too. They worked in clothing stores, restaurants, and thrift shops. "I wanted them to know that everything takes hard work," Donna explained. "Nobody's going to give you anything. You work for it." She's very proud of her daughters' work ethic, which she believes resulted from those busy years. She recalls with amusement the practical ways they sometimes put their creativity to use. After Este read that waitresses with Southern accents out earned the others, she affected a winning drawl. Her apron pockets bulged with tips.

The parents expected the girls to attend college. Este went to UCLA and graduated in just two years with a degree in ethnomusicology. Danielle enrolled at UCLA, but at nineteen she had an opportunity to go on tour with Jenny Lewis's band. She was determined to go.

Donna was adamant that she would not, and the conflict, which Donna describes as the hardest time in their mother-daughter relationship, played out over a long weekend. Donna knew she would never be able to sleep if the daughter she still saw as a child was out on the road, in unknown places with unknown people. She was too young! Finish school. Wait. Don't go! Moti thought Danielle would be just fine and acted as arbitrator. In the end, after many tears, Donna trusted his instincts. And Danielle went off on tour. After her stint with Lewis, she played some shows with Julian Casablancas and with CeeLo Green. And Donna survived.

The sisters were always very close and looked out for each other. They weren't as competitive as some sisters are; they found a way to blend their roles as well as their voices. They wrote and played music together and occasionally ventured out to play in small rooms around the Valley. Donna laughs as she tells of their very first show, which took place in 2007 at a clown museum in North Hollywood. Artists had to guarantee the sale of 130 tickets—"pay to play," Donna calls it. Donna and Moti bought most of the tickets and gave them to the girls' friends. There, in the strangest atmosphere imaginable, with "crazy clown heads all over the walls," HAIM entertained their parents and their friends with exciting original music. "They were amazing, just amazing!" says Donna.

Other dates were less successful. When they played the Satellite, Alana wasn't yet sixteen so liquor laws required that Donna and Alana stand on the sidewalk outside the club until it was time for the band to jump onstage to play, then make a quick exit after the last note. Sometimes they would show up as the first of several opening bands and play for three or four people. Perhaps it built character and stamina. At least it was good practice. Donna and Moti were the band's full staff—managers, roadies, drivers—and, of course, they loved it.

When the band resumed after Danielle's time on the road, momentum picked up. They hired a drummer, Dash Hutton, and released a three-song EP on their website. The music world noticed. They played South by Southwest (a major music festival in Austin), signed with a record label, and began to tour, opening for big names like Mumford and Sons and Florence and the Machine. They were a huge success in the

UK, topping charts and winning awards there before their home audiences started to catch on. They were clearly launched.

And now it was time for Donna and Moti to step back. They were no longer needed as managers, roadies, or merchandise vendors. The parents who had encouraged and played with their girls were now a part of the audience. Donna had to let go of all three. "It's hard to have all your kids out on the road, but at least they're together. They're like a wolf pack, watching out for each other, taking care of each other. That's how they were raised." She finds comfort in that.

Donna and Moti travel with HAIM as often as their real estate business will allow. They are learning as they go. Sometimes fans cause tense moments by jumping onstage or tossing water bottles near the electrical equipment. But when that happened recently, Alana stepped to the front of the stage and said, "Dude, didn't your mother teach you to be nice to women? That wasn't a very nice thing to do!"

There have been trips to Australia, Japan, and England, and a special trip out to the desert to the Coachella Festival. Donna took her eighty-two-year-old father along so he could see the girls play. It's an important memory for all of them because he died only a few months later.

Good neighbors

HAIM,
Foo Fighters &
Stevie Nicks
at the Forum

HAIM at the
Staples Center

Recently the Haims booked the Troubadour to honor the memory of an old friend: actress and musician Sammi Kane Kraft, who died in a car accident in 2012 at age twenty. The Troubadour, a club in West Hollywood, was significant in HAIM's early days. It was where a manager-to-be first heard them, where they played to an empty room while fans of other, more-noted bands sauntered in, where Donna sold T-shirts in the lobby and Moti hauled equipment onstage. They called the event Sam Jam and donated all the profits to Our House, a counseling center that helps grieving families deal with devastating losses. The show sold out in minutes. HAIM played all the hits their fans love, invited Jenny Lewis and other notable acts to join them, and surprised the audience by reuniting Rockinhaim. Donna and Moti came to the stage to thunderous applause, then rocked the house with "Johnny B. Goode" and

"Mustang Sally." Moti played a two-minute drum solo. The evening was a tribute in so many ways.

Donna loves that the girls haven't changed. They love playing together onstage. They love seeing old friends in the audience, even in the larger arenas they now play. She says, "Oh, they can afford better shoes now, and they don't buy all their clothes in thrift shops, but they are still compassionate and appreciative of the gifts their lives have yielded."

HAIM's first album, *Days Are Gone,* earned them *New Musical Express* magazine's award for Best International Band in 2014. That summer they toured festivals in every European country and played throughout the United States. They were nominated for Best New Artist at the 2015 Grammy Awards but lost to Sam Smith. They opened for Taylor Swift's *1989* tour in several East Coast cities and for five sold-out nights at the Staples Center in LA. I was there for one of the shows and got to see HAIM rock that cavernous arena with their youthful, ebullient, musical genius. Afterward I met them backstage. They are warm, funny, affable young women. No wonder Donna is so proud! They told me they are seriously intent on babysitting my three little granddaughters to ensure that the next generation will have a new hard-rocking sister act.

A month later, David invited HAIM to take the stage at the Forum with the Foo Fighters and Stevie Nicks for a fantastic rendering of "Stop Draggin' My Heart Around." Donna, Moti, and I were beside ourselves with joy and love and, well, just the *fun* of all this. The backstage scene was like a big family reunion.

In 2017 HAIM's long-anticipated second album will be released, supported by extensive US and European tours. Donna and Moti will join them when they can and, when they can't, will check in often with reminders to call home and be safe. "Are your doors locked?" is Moti's usual conversation starter. HAIM will be making music together for a very long time, in perfect three-part harmony assuring the legacy of this extraordinary musical family.

GARY LEE WEINRIB

Born: July 29, 1953, in Willowdale, Toronto, Canada

Rush (1968–2015): Lead vocals, bass guitar, keyboard, synthesizers

Genre: Rock

First Album: *Rush* (1974)

MARY WEINRIB

Mother of Geddy Lee
(Rush)

DARK CLOUDS LOOMED ABOVE the town of Starachowice, Poland, as a fourteen-year-old girl sat on the front steps of her house listening to the fearful, hushed tones of the neighborhood men pondering their uncertain future. War was imminent. It would destroy most of their lives and shape the future of the young girl who heard her father and his friends wonder when the Germans would come.

Manya Rubenstein, the mother of Rush's Geddy Lee, had lived in Starachowice for most of her life. A small town seventy-five miles south of Warsaw, it was known for its munitions factory and copper and iron foundries. The population included five thousand Jews.

On September 1, 1939, the first day of the German invasion, the Nazis bombed the town in a failed attempt to disable the munitions factory. Soldiers marched in, looting stores, beating and killing Jews, and burning the synagogue that held their sacred books and scrolls. A curfew was enforced, property confiscated, and the yellow Star of David required to be worn on the arm of every Jew. For two years the remaining Jews, as well as those from surrounding towns, were enclosed in the ghetto near the center of town. Due to overcrowding and a meager food supply, malnutrition and disease killed many of them. During this time Manya's father was seized by the SS, shot, and killed as she watched.

The criminality and resulting terror escalated in 1942 when the Germans ordered all the residents of the ghetto into the marketplace.

SS troops separated the old from the young, the frail from the strong, for what they termed "resettlement." Forty-five hundred Jews were deported to Treblinka death camp, where they disappeared forever. The rest were packed into railcars with no food or water and transported to Auschwitz, where an immediate selection took place. A brutish SS guard designated "Right, left, right" as he assessed the long line of prisoners. Those on the right were deemed strong enough to work; those on the left would go to the gas chambers. Manya, naturally small and frail and completely terrified, was sent to the left, her mother and sister to the right. Her horrified mother sneaked behind the line and pulled her daughter to the right, saving her life. Those on the left vanished.

In the Starachowice ghetto, Manya had been assigned to the brick-making ovens. For long hours she stood barefoot in the mud, taking bricks out of the kilns and putting them on racks to dry, her feet uncovered because a German guard had admired her boots, her only shoes, and confiscated them. After exhausting days at the brick oven, a meal of thin soup and one piece of bread was the only nourishment provided. The soup made Manya sick, so she sustained herself with the daily chunk of bread and became even more frail. She had learned, though, that she must always appear to be strong and able. At Auschwitz her job was loading cargo, a task that required strength and energy, and she worked hard to fulfill her tasks, to avoid standing out and looking like the sick, weak child she was.

There was one thing to look forward to each day. A handsome young forklift driver caught her eye, and they began a silent, forbidden romance with what she calls a "special communication." He was Morris Weinrib, the love of her life. But he was soon to be transferred to Dachau. One more loss!

In 1944 Auschwitz was evacuated as the Russian army advanced. Most prisoners, including Manya, her mother, and her sister, were transferred to Bergen-Belsen, a camp located in northern Germany, where overcrowding resulted in astounding death rates for the 60,000 prisoners who passed through the gates. Upon liberation, in April 1945, only 2,560 Jews had survived. Anne Frank was one who didn't make it. She died there in March 1945. The three Rubenstein women were among the few survivors.

Morris, Mary, Susie, & Geddy

Geddy & sister Susie

Isolated from the world for so long, convinced that civilization had ceased to exist, many of the survivors stayed at Bergen-Belsen, which was converted to a relocation camp, until they could find a future home. Morris went there to search for Manya. They were reunited and married in 1946 at the former German Officers' Club, and they decided to emigrate to Canada. Manya would have new hope, a new life, and a new name, Mary Weinrib.

In 2013, more than sixty-five years later, I traveled to Toronto, Canada, to meet Mary and learn the story of the two Holocaust survivors who arrived there with nothing but each other yet managed to build a life and a family, and to give the world a Hall of Fame rock-star son, Geddy Lee.

The street where Mary lives is charming, lined with tall trees that warn of early winter and bend in a gusty wind. But Mary's apartment is warm and cozy, and she is at the door to greet me. Mary is a beautiful woman. Her smooth, almost unlined face belies her age—she turned ninety in 2015—and her bright smile and welcoming demeanor promised a long, pleasant conversation and an unforgettable afternoon.

She tells of the decisions she and Morris faced after liberation. Where would they go? What would they do? Their homeland had been ravaged by war. Europe had been torn apart and reshaped, but how would there be peace? And would there ever be safety and stability? All was unknown. They had been hidden behind bars and gates for so long that the outside world was a mystery to them. Their schooling had been cut short, their families decimated, and they owned nothing.

Susie Gitajn, Mary's daughter, who joined us, says they have always understood the connection between perseverance and survival, and she believes it was those strong values that they brought to their new world.

Mary and Morris found jobs in a sewing factory in Canada, where each earned twenty-five cents an hour. "It would have been an easy job," Mary says, "if I had known how to sew!" And she smiles at the nerve she had asking her boss to teach her. He did, and she became the most proficient worker on the floor. Some years later Morris would find his talents put to best use working in and later owning the Times Square Discount Store in Newmarket, a suburb of Toronto. A popular, prosperous store, it was this business that made it possible for him to provide for the three children they would have.

The 1950s were indeed happy days. Susie, the first child, was born in 1951, followed by Gary two years later. Allan was born in 1960. By then they lived in a two-story house in Toronto with a kosher kitchen for Grandmother in the basement and a large recreation room that Morris built.

Both Susie and Geddy, whom I spoke to later, tell of happy, uncomplicated early-childhood days. School success was a major priority, and Mary was home with the children to ensure that all schoolwork was done and done well. Theirs was a strict, religious household, though it was never Orthodox enough to please Grandmother, who tried hard to hold to traditional Jewish practices and values. It may have been difficult for the children at times, but Geddy credits his grandmother's determined efforts with showing them how strong a family is when they are all together.

The children had neighborhood friends and school activities. Sundays were set aside for family time. Often they drove to a nearby park, where they swam and picnicked during the day. As night fell they watched the drive-in movie there, enjoying the kind of wholesome family fun that sadly disappeared soon after.

Mary was insistent that her sons would become doctors or scientists and "do big things in the world." The education that had been stolen from her and Morris was available now for her children and it was not to be wasted. Geddy was a good student, often excelling and being promoted to enrichment classes. Life was not easy, but dreams for the future were bright.

The pleasant stability ended abruptly in 1965, when Morris died suddenly and unexpectedly at home. One minute he and Mary had been chatting about the events of the day, the next he was gone. And a new struggle for survival began. Mary was left alone with three young children, a strict, religious mother, a large house, and a store she knew nothing about.

Stunned and depressed by the unexpected tragedy, she broke down. Doctors gave her pills to help her deal with the shock, but she slept and cried for two weeks. She could not leave her bed. Life without Morris was unimaginable, just too hard.

Mary recalls a night when Geddy heard her crying and came to her room. He sat on the edge of her bed and said, "Mommy, I know why you're crying; you don't know what to do. Daddy would want you to go and open the store . . . because he made it."

He was twelve years old.

Mary threw the pills away, got out of bed, made breakfast for the children, took them to school, and opened the store. She learned how to operate the cash register and how to order, price, and stock merchandise. She took over. Her children often worked with her, and years later their children did, too.

For a long time after his death, Mary talked to her husband as she drove home from work. She told him of the decisions she was struggling with, what to buy, how to stock and sell. And she talked to him about her concerns for the children. The answers came. She managed. Except for one thing. The scientist-doctor future she had envisioned for her first son was looking unlikely. Geddy had already determined that his life would be in music.

Morris had played the balalaika in his youth but had never mentioned it to the children and they knew of no musical tradition in the family. It surprised everyone when Morris had a piano delivered to the house. Susie, as the eldest, was designated the family pianist and lessons were arranged. She hated every minute of the ordeal, still grimacing as she recalls her inability to coax a song from the keys. After their session one day, the teacher had tea with Mary in the kitchen. Soon the sounds of lilting chords and rhythms came from the piano in the other room. It was that day's lesson being played perfectly.

And it was Geddy at the piano! He had learned the piece as he lay on the floor listening to the lesson. They were amazed at his performance. He was a natural. But Geddy already knew that he would turn his musical ear to guitar. He was drawn to the chords and energy of rock and roll. He needed now to convince his mother to buy him an instrument.

One day, after a long shift at the store, Mary turned to him with praise: "Geddy, you have worked so hard. How can I repay you?" He had a quick answer, and two days later, a guitar. He taught himself to play, his musical ear quickly translating the sounds of his idols, Eric Clapton and Cream, to his own guitar. He also loved Neil Young, Jefferson Airplane, and the Yardbirds, and he imitated their chords until he could play complete songs. His first was "For Your Love." At fourteen he knew he wanted nothing more than a life in music. His friends joined him, and Rush was formed right there, in his basement. Mary was about to find out what happens when a musician in the making is the child who was supposed to be a doctor—the future she had dreamed of for years. But although other professions might gradually or subtly inspire children, music is a calling that doesn't call softly or politely. It screams insistently. The musician WILL find a way.

After that, Mary recalls, "Day and night, night and day he was playing." He gathered friends in the basement, and the once quiet house became a source of despair for the neighbors and Grandmother as loud rock music blasted down the block. A truce was reached with the neighbors when an eight o'clock curfew was agreed to, but the infuriated Grandmother was not so easily ameliorated. She eventually moved out, to the quieter home of her other daughter.

Mary shakes her head at the memories of those difficult times. She was in the middle, trying to keep peace between her hard-rocking son and her kosher-keeping mother. "I survived the war and the concentration camps," she recalls. "But I also survived the war in my house. When I was a kid, I didn't know I'm gonna come out alive. But I knew I'd come out of this alive . . . bruised, but alive!"

The wars didn't end there. There was also the Battle of the Hair, a global parental nightmare that pervaded the '60s and '70s. Mary tells of the rudeness of friends and family, who goaded her constantly. "How do you let your son walk around like this? Look at him!" She decided to do them all a favor and planned to surreptitiously cut his hair. But as she approached, scissors in hand, he woke up and she backed off. A bit ashamed and completely helpless, she declared, "OK, that's it. I don't care if he has hair to his knees." And she never criticized his hair again. By the way, the hair-knee gap narrowed.

The final battle was the school war. Geddy's early successes had led Mary to expect high school graduation and then university. It seemed certain until, as Geddy says, he became "distracted." His talent exploded and Rush got good fast. They were asked to play parties and high school dances, even small clubs. They went to school, then rehearsed, then played gigs at night, sacrificing sleep and homework.

Geddy told me the story of his high school counselor, Mr. Woodhouse, who worked tirelessly with Geddy to try to arrange his schedule to accommodate the needs of school and band. They scheduled all his classes in the morning to allow more flexibility for afternoon and evening events. But Rush was in demand now, and the evenings were filled with the business of preparing for, getting to, and playing gigs. There was little time for sleep. And sadly it often meant those morning classes were missed. Geddy felt so guilty. He knew he was causing anguish for Mary, and he hated knowing he was hurting her. He told Mr. Woodhouse that he felt "really torn." He had tried everything to stay in school and would not drop out without his mother's permission, even though it was officially unnecessary.

It was then, during Geddy's senior year, that the counselor called Mary for a conference. She recalls the painful day when the counselor and principal recommended that her future doctor drop out of school. They told her they were aware of his talent and commitment to the band, and they understood that he couldn't continue to succeed in both school and music. Mary remembers the words. "They said, 'Geddy is gonna go far. You have to give him the chance.'"

She agreed. But it hurt.

Geddy tells of the painful aftermath. His mother wouldn't speak to him for weeks. He knew his decision didn't make sense to her. She accepted it, but she certainly wasn't happy with it. "In fact," Geddy

Mary & Geddy

So proud

says, "it wasn't till she saw me on TV that she realized I was succeeding in something!"

Mary, on the other hand, says she began to understand how good her son was when she went to see his shows. Susie took her to an early gig at a tiny club upstairs from Georgia's Spaghetti House. "Surprisingly," she says, "I liked it! He and his long hair belonged on that stage."

When the first Rush album was released, Mary plastered the windows of her store with Rush posters and gave albums away to any kids who wanted them but didn't have the money to buy them. She even advised the kids to play the record at school!

This was in 1974, a year when the top of the charts featured Barbra Streisand, the Jackson 5, Elton John, Cat Stevens, and the Carpenters. Rock and roll was not yet the dominant sound, but times were changing. New, loud, vibrant music played by trios and quartets of masterful guitarists and powerhouse drummers was vying for the attention of a world full of young, eager listeners.

There was another Mary–Gary Lee adjustment. Mary's accented version of her son's name—Geddy Lee—had been picked up by his friends, and it caught on. Eventually he changed it legally. Mary named her son twice.

And so it began. Rush produced twenty-one albums in their forty-year career, garnering countless gold and platinum records and earning high honors. In 1996 all three members of the band became Officers of the Order of Canada, and in 2012 they received the Governor General's Performing Arts Award for Lifetime Artistic Achievement. Canada invited them into their Music Hall of Fame in 1994, and the Rock and Roll Hall of Fame finally got around to inducting them in 2013. It was a proud moment for my own son, Dave Grohl, when he was chosen to give the induction speech. He met Mary that night and called me right away. "Mom, you must meet her! You two could be such good friends!" He was absolutely right.

The many honors and accolades have made Mary very proud of her son's "big mind doing big things, going to big places." She is even more proud of the man her son has become, proud that he is still in love with Nancy, the woman he married over thirty years ago, proud of his devotion to his son and daughter . . . and now to a new grandson.

In 1995 Geddy, Susie, Allan, and Mary traveled to Germany for the fiftieth anniversary of the liberation of Bergen-Belsen. It was an emotional reunion of survivors, and the last stories that Mary had kept to herself poured out. Somehow she felt victorious rather than vengeful. She had survived; the Nazis had not. Geddy says, "It was a huge moment for her. She realized she had won the war. She was a different person after that, as if there had been some kind of closure."

Side of the stage
rock moms

Ten years earlier Geddy had told Neil Peart, the Rush drummer and lyricist, stories his mother had told of the camps, and in response Neil wrote "Red Sector A" for their album *Grace Under Pressure*. In a powerful vignette about fear and urgency, he evoked the images of "ragged lines of ragged gray," of "skeletons shuffling," and of Mary clutching a wire fence. Now Mary was able to walk straight and tall and leave those images behind.

Twenty years on, this remarkably vibrant and beautiful great-grandmother lives in Toronto with her family close by. Susie is her mother's "right hand." She and her daughter Erin are there to help whenever Mary needs them. When Geddy is in town, mother and son have a regular Saturday date: a walk, lunch in a restaurant, perhaps a Blue Jays game. Allan takes her to dinner one night a week.

Summer vacations find the whole family gathered at Geddy's summer cottage, where they swim in the lake, play tennis, cook for each other, play board games, and catch up on events of the past year. Mary gets the chance to visit with Geddy's son, Julian, the doctor she can finally brag about. He earned a PhD in higher education at the University of Toronto and now serves there as special projects officer in the Office of the Vice-President and Provost.

Fortune has been doubly kind. On June 12, 2014, Geddy accepted an honorary PhD from Nipissing University, and he, in turn, honored Mary in his heartfelt speech. He started by saying, "Finally! My mother's dream comes true. She has a doctor for a son! Oy vey!" He briefly referred to his own journey but said it "pales in comparison to my mother's journey. I would not be here without her courage and incredible desire to succeed in life despite hardships and real peril. My mother understood the true meaning of perseverance, surviving the horrors of her imprisonment, coming to a new country, learning a new language . . . without the luxury of choice." Dr. Geddy Lee ended the acceptance of his doctorate with, "I dedicate this to my mom, Mary Weinrib."

Oy vey, indeed.

VIGNETTE #5

HAVE RHINESTONES, WILL TRAVEL

The life of a rock-star mom is occasionally decorated with a bit of glitter and glamour. Once or twice a year I visit the few shops that carry chic, formal garb in sizes that have double digits (rarities in LA) and spend a terrifying amount of money on an outfit. I consistently break the only-wear-it-once rule, but I happily accept that dressing up is part of the fun of special events. Realistically, I know that it doesn't matter very much what I am wearing. All eyes will go to Jordyn, my daughter-in-law, who is always the most beautiful woman in the room. And my son will cause a few camera clicks as well. So the old lady tottering after them is safely out of view. I could wear sweatpants and fuzzy slippers and escape notice. But that wouldn't be much fun.

A bit of silk, a sequin or two, eye shadow that somebody else applies, and red, red lipstick. Showtime! A driver will appear at my door, escort me to a shiny black town car, and I will be off to a great evening at the Grammys, the Kennedy Center Honors, the Gershwin Prize, or the Rock and Roll Hall of Fame extravaganza. I still pinch myself. Am I really part of this? Thrilling!

My favorite event is the Kennedy Center Honors annual presentation. On one prestigious evening each year, a few of our best and brightest artists are chosen to be honored for their lifetime of work in the arts. Other artists perform their music and sing their praises as these icons receive medals. The event is filled with newsmakers and newswriters. There's Aretha Franklin! Look, Charlie Rose and Stephen Colbert just walked by! Itzhak Perlman is right in front of me! One can name just about every person there. Everyone is excited by the beautifully produced segments of film clips, surprising musical combinations, and heartfelt speeches. After these, all eyes turn to the first balcony, where the president and his wife are seated next to the honorees. There are many standing ovations.

The event also includes an afternoon reception at the White House, where I've followed Kid Rock in line to meet the First Family and later chatted with Nancy Pelosi as her husband slid down a banister.

The year that Led Zeppelin received the honor and David was invited to play in the ceremony, the event overlapped with the Christmas season. The White House was adorned with holiday decorations. Cedar garlands swooped gracefully over sparkling topiaries and specially themed trees. Dozens of volunteers had worked for months under the keen eye of Mrs. Obama to create unique holiday tableaus in each room so that the oohs and aahs continued as we were escorted from one room to another. The final stop, the reception room, held canapés, sweets, and champagne—and the magnificent White House cake was on display, a sumptuously frosted dollhouse mansion. It was a fabulous party and certainly worth the price of a new outfit.

On June 2, 2010, in the East Room of the White House, Sir Paul McCartney received the third Gershwin Prize, an honor given by the Library of Congress to commemorate a composer for his or her lifetime contribution to popular music. The previous winners were Paul Simon and Stevie Wonder. Paul chose a roster of musicians and assigned each of them one of his songs for the show. Emmylou Harris, Elvis Costello, Herbie Hancock, and other greats serenaded the First Family, who were seated in the front row. Paul went from audience to stage throughout the program. He joined Stevie Wonder for "Ebony and Ivory," which had many of us in tears, then sat to hear Corinne Bailey Rae do a stirring rendition of "Blackbird." The president sang along to "Michelle," and the Obama girls were delighted when the Jonas Brothers sang "Drive My Car." There was a little something for everyone in the audience.

My favorite part, of course, was when my son, David, decked out in a navy Sgt. Pepper jacket, came to the stage to do "Band on the Run." He was just two feet from Sir Paul McCartney and the President of the United States of America! I was sure that would be his crowning achievement and the best time I would ever have. It was an unforgettable night.

Another moment to remember, and no rhinestones were required, was an invitation to a garden reception at the American Ambassador's house in London, where David and the Foo Fighters would help Prince Harry open the Invictus Games week. The charming prince must have said something terribly funny, but I admit to being so enchanted I don't recall a word.

Perhaps the biggest event, at least in my life story, occurred in 2014, when my son was inducted into the Rock and Roll Hall of Fame as one of the members of Nirvana. I looked forward to a reunion with the Seattle folks, a close-knit group of very young light and sound techs and radio people. I couldn't wait to see Wendy Cobain O'Connor, Kurt's mother, even as I worried that the emotion of hearing tributes to the son she had lost would be a heavy emotional burden. I wanted to be there for her.

And then it began. The darkened stage suddenly lit up to reveal a full-stage poster of Nirvana, those three sweet young faces in the spotlight again. I dissolved in tears. It was a moment I hadn't predicted. It stunned me. Twenty years had passed, but that dizzying fame and the pain of Kurt's suicide that forced an early end to a time like no other flooded back.

After that rough start, the show became a wonderful reminder of the powerful music they played. David was back on drums, pounding harder than ever, hair flying straight up. Krist was playing bass and accordion with his signature quirky moves, and Pat Smear was grinning as he danced with his guitar. We all had a lovely, happy time singing along. Wendy even danced. Afterward, well after midnight, we went to a club David had rented, where Nirvana played for the last time until five in the morning.

The honor of being in the Hall of Fame and the trophies that came with it are treasures. But it was the presence of that first family—many of whom are still with David, who came to honor their old friends, and who remembered how it was when it all began—that made the night so magical and special.

And until David wins Father of the Year (which he richly deserves) or a Nobel Prize (after Dylan, who knows?), I think that will be quite enough.

Meeting Prince Charming

ADAM NOAH LEVINE

Born: March 18, 1979, in Los Angeles, California

Maroon 5 (2001–present): Vocals, guitar, bass, piano, drums

Kara's Flowers (1994–2001)

Genre: Pop rock

First Album: *Songs About Jane* (2002)

PATSY NOAH

Mother of Adam Levine
(Maroon 5)

I FIRST SAW PATSY NOAH, rolling her eyes and smiling ever so patiently at Sharon Feldstein, Jonah Hill's hilariously outspoken mother, in a television public-service announcement for President Obama's Affordable Care Act. They were joined by the similarly beleaguered mothers of Alicia Keys and Jennifer Lopez in a short, humorous plea to young people to sign up for health insurance. "Do you want your mothers to have a nervous breakdown?" Sharon bemoans. "After all we've done for you!" She and Patsy, friends for years, go on to describe their sons' devilish pranks before the video clip ends with Michelle Obama saying, "We nag you because we love you."

It's a peek behind the curtain at the unrecognized mothers of world-recognized stars. And it's the same conversation any two or three old friends might have about their kids who have been "a handful," as we say, and who can still benefit from a bit of advice from Mom.

That same humor, subtle and friendly, punctuated the conversation I had with Patsy in her Brentwood apartment in Los Angeles. Despite our age difference—she was born the year I graduated high school—we had more in common than most people meeting for the first time: our "other coast" childhoods, our work in education, and our rock-star mom designations. Patsy is the mother of Adam Levine of Maroon 5.

This was my first visit to Brentwood, an upscale area on the west side of LA. I had expected a Beverly Hills vibe: designer shops, huge mansions, gates everywhere. Instead I drove by bakeries, delis, cafes, and small markets in the friendly-looking village area just a few blocks from Patsy's apartment.

Dressed in jeans and a neat navy buttoned shirt, she showed me into her small, cozy apartment. Family photos decorate the walls that surround a comfortable sectional couch, where Patsy invited me to join her. She's a petite, young-looking woman, her short gray hair the only clue to her grandmother status. I found her instantly affable and charming and was pleased that she didn't once roll her eyes as she told me her story.

Born in 1955 in New York City and raised in New Rochelle, New York, Patsy grew up in a family of creative, successful writers. Her father, Robert M. Noah, was a TV writer and producer responsible for many of the game shows that were the craze of the '60s. Remember *Match Game*? It was introduced in 1962 and was syndicated, revised, reworked, and reborn for many years after, well into the next millennium. Robert is still consulting and working on projects.

Patsy's older brother, Peter, spent some time in a band writing terrific songs, according to Patsy. He is now a successful TV writer as well. Patsy's other brother, Timothy Noah, might be a name or face you recognize—he's a respected Washington journalist. He married Marjorie Williams, an editor at the *Washington Post* and a contributor to *Vanity Fair*. In her short forty-seven-year lifespan she wrote remarkably astute profiles of the political power brokers in DC, which Timothy published in posthumous collections after her death. *The Woman at the Washington Zoo* and *Reputation: Portraits in Power* are two brilliant must-reads.

The Noahs were typical kids, enjoying school and friends in a middle-class suburb of the big city until their father announced that they would move to Los Angeles. Patsy began high school in an unfamiliar place, bereft of her old friends and lacking in self-confidence. She decided to "just get through it" and focus on the college life at Berkeley that lay ahead. Soon after arriving at "Berzerkeley," as one alum has called the epicenter of the '60s student uprisings, she met Fred Levine, a law student. They married and moved to Los Angeles, where their first son, Adam, was born a year later.

At twenty-four Patsy was a new mother and wife in a sprawling city where her husband was devoting his time to creating the family busi-

Adam & Patsy

Sports Star

ness. She recalls this in a matter-of-fact manner, but it meant that she and son Adam "kind of grew up together." She believes that their close bond, "almost a spiritual connection, a mother-son ESP," was forged in those early days. Fred worked hard on what is now a well-known chain of clothing stores called M.Fredric, and Patsy and Adam explored their new territory together.

Adam talked early (and often) and like every other rock-star baby I've learned about had a supersized energy level. "Drove me crazy!" Patsy laughs. "He was a handful, no question!" There was, though, "that spark, that kind of twinkle in his eye" that assured that he was more lovable than exasperating. His astute mother, used to the creative, energetic men in her family, recognized the spark and in later years would be drawn to the students at the school where she worked who exuded that same rebellious energy force. They, in turn, sought her out.

We had that in common and digressed a bit to talk about our experiences as educators. I recalled the memorable former students who challenged me and all the boundaries they could, often with happy results. In one of my AP English 12 classes, for example, two brilliant bad boys created a moment to remember. Having slogged through several scenes of *Othello,* they bounded into the classroom and announced that they might have found a better way to present the vagaries of the unfortunate Moor and his diabolical advisor. "Go for it!" I said, and relaxed in my chair as they delivered a twenty-minute rap version of the difficult

Shakespeare play. It was brilliant. And unforgettable. Last year for my birthday, Rapper #1 gave me a copy of the manuscript. He had saved it for over twenty years!

Adam's creative spark didn't fully ignite until music became the center of his life. There were some trying times ahead for the classically educated mother because "Adam had different ideas about school. He never worked hard except for the special teachers he didn't want to disappoint." He loved sports, though, and was a good athlete. The basketball programs at his schools kept him happy and involved.

Patsy researched the hundreds of school options available in the Los Angeles area, learning about the different methods and alternative structures on offer—magnet schools, charter schools, private schools, religious schools, and traditional neighborhood schools. She decided to enroll the four-year-old Adam in the Center for Early Education, which she described as "very progressive," the perfect place for curious, energetic children. Emphasis on academics is balanced by sports and music programs that involve all students. A yearly Olympics event excited the athletic Adam. He both competed in the sporting events and entertained in the opening and closing ceremonies. Patsy noted that these activities absorbed some of his energy, making it possible for him to succeed academically. To this day he is appreciative of that balanced approach. Maroon 5 will play at a benefit for the school, a guarantee of sold-out ticket status.

When Adam was five his brother, Michael, was born. Now Patsy had two hyperactive, creative, beautiful boys to keep her endlessly busy. Two years later, she and Fred divorced and she got a job at Brentwood School.

As I looked back on our conversation, I noticed the remarkable absence of negativity and self-pity in Patsy's remembrances. She has chosen to spend her energy taking care and taking note. There's been no time for self-indulgence. We both agree that single parenting gets a bad rap. During Patsy's years as a single mother, she found it liberating to make decisions without consultation, to plan their daily activities and know she was free to revise those plans. Some women thrive in that freedom.

All that changed when she remarried, but her two very protective sons were able to accept a blended family—a stepfather and a stepsister—when Patsy's new husband, Phil Bartolf, and his daughter, Julia, joined the family. They all learned to get along, adjusting nicely to each other.

After his elementary and middle school years, Adam chose to go to Brentwood School, where Patsy by then worked as an admissions counselor. He chose it because he admired the strong sports program, but Patsy had concerns that it might not be the right fit for her son. Nevertheless, she allowed him to decide. Brentwood, a private, college-prep high school, is "highly academic, but not punishing," according to Patsy. The school is proud that 100 percent of its graduates are admitted to college, and the staff works creatively to assure that every student finds a suitable school placement.

For a while the Brentwood sports program kept Adam happy and involved. Then, when he was fourteen, he told his mother he had something very serious he wanted to talk to her about. "Sit down," he said, preparing her for what she thought would be "profoundly scary" news.

"I'm giving up sports."

Patsy's first, silent reaction was "That's it?" But she knew he had reached a serious turning point and that her basketball-mom life was about to change to that of band mom: driver, roadie, first fan. His energy and focus would shift to music. The fourteen-year-old saw his future. Neither Adam's mother nor his teachers applauded the change. Once sports were taken out of the equation, they were challenged to find ways to keep him interested and in school. It wasn't easy.

When Patsy and Adam look back on his school years, they agree that several teachers were significant. The earliest, "Adam's true inspiration," Patsy tells me, was Gar, an elementary teacher who was the first to discover Adam's singing voice. Adam didn't believe he could sing well, but he will never forget the persistence and encouragement of his teacher. Many years after the death of this influential mentor, Adam holds his memory close.

Dennis Castaneres, a middle school teacher, is also remembered favorably. He "guided the boys toward their passion," the grateful mother recalls. Sometimes having just one instructor each day who provides an island of safety for a creative child who is floundering in his other classes is enough to get him through. Those rare teachers are never forgotten.

Adam had been "a willful, impulsive little boy," traits Patsy noted were "strengths when it came to competitive sports but an impediment to having a smooth day at home." He stubbornly resisted homework and deadlines. The mother-son relationship was tested but survived—perhaps, Patsy believes, because of another teacher who made a difference.

Brentwood ninth graders were required to select a school activity, so Adam and three other boys formed a pep band. They were expected to play at pep rallies and sporting events, of course. But Adam and his pals wanted to make it a rock band, and their teacher agreed to their plan. Patsy credits the "fantastic teacher at a very straitlaced school" who allowed them to defy expectations—to eschew the tuba and trumpets and rock the rallies! They also played at dances and other events and became very popular. "They broke the mold," Patsy says. This pep band was the first version of Kara's Flowers and soon became the most important thing in Adam's life. The early piano lessons he had resisted and the guitar instruction that replaced them were all in the past. He now had a band.

Kara's Flowers performed wherever they could. They played at school events and booked shows at the Troubadour, the Viper Room, the Roxy, and Whisky a Go Go. In those pre-Internet days newbie bands had to make their own flyers and distribute them all over town in order to fill the clubs where they played. They learned how to do it all: book shows and publicize them, and then rehearse and perform. "That's what both my boys did," Patsy says of her self-sufficient children.

Adam's brother, Michael, Patsy's second self-starter son, is interested in acting and musical theater and, according to his supremely proud mother, has a beautiful voice. When he was eleven he announced, "I have an audition at the Morgan-Wixson Theatre in Santa Monica on Wednesday at seven. Can you drive me?"

This was news to Patsy, who saw herself as an anti–stage mom. But her independent fifth-grade son explained that he had missed the audition but had talked the director into inviting him for callbacks. "My kids just had a knack for knowing how to manage themselves," she noted. Although all Patsy had to do was drive the car, she was aware that both sons had chosen their futures and that she was "just along for the ride," helpless to intervene. When you parent a gifted child, Patsy believes, you need to be realistic. "I knew I didn't have anything to do with it except to allow it. With Adam I knew there was no way I could stop him, so it was an argument I wasn't willing to have."

Adam went to French Woods Camp in the Catskills for five summers, starting at age twelve. It was a performing arts camp specializing in musical theater and orchestra. But there was also a Rock Shop, and it was there that Adam and some of his California friends lived happily, forming a band and going to small towns nearby to play at clubs and cafes, gaining onstage experience in a relaxed, welcoming atmosphere.

After Adam's graduation from Brentwood, the school's promise of a suitable college placement led him and his bandmate Jesse Carmichael to Five Towns College, an obscure school in Long Island, New York. But by that time their band, Kara's Flowers, had made a record and they deferred enrollment, opting instead to go on a van tour.

They played wherever they could get a gig, but came home "with their tails between their legs," as Patsy puts it. The small record label did not support the record and soon dropped them. They had made some money, though, and that bought them time to go their separate ways for a short time, some of the members to UCLA and Adam and Jesse to Five Towns. Patsy thinks that brief Long Island interim opened her son to a variety of sounds and styles of music that later affected his music.

After a semester Adam and Jesse changed the band's name from Kara's Flowers to Maroon 5, came back to LA, and hired Jordan Feldstein, Jonah Hill's older brother, as their manager. Patsy credits him with being "the brains behind all of this," and notes that he is still with Maroon 5 over a decade later. *Songs About Jane*, released in 2002, was the band's first multiplatinum record. It led to four more albums, three Grammys, four *Billboard* Music Awards, and sold-out arenas. The "Best New Artist" band catapulted to fame and fortune.

Patsy and Adam still remember the uncertainty of early performances. She recalls her son standing with his back to the audience at the Troubadour because he was so nervous. He recalls the trauma of looking at his acne-spotted face in the mirror and thinking how ugly he was. He couldn't have known then that he would be named *People* magazine's Sexiest Man Alive when he reached his thirties. He couldn't have foreseen that he would act on TV and in movies and be a part of this decade's most popular TV music show, *The Voice,* where he's held a seat since 2011.

At times Adam and Patsy reflect on the difficult days, the early failures and setbacks. Adam now appreciates this part of the process, especially as he sees young stars plummet from too-much-too-soon fame to heartbreaking childish behaviors and embarrassing tabloid coverage. Patsy believes that "failures build endurance, and that creates the confidence that is necessary for real success."

Mother and son agree that success has an upside and a downside. Early on, Adam issued an open invitation for his mother to accompany him on tour, and Patsy has joined him in many of the cities and countries he's traveled to. The backstage scenes have allowed her to meet some of her own music idols, including Sting, Stevie Nicks, and Bono. In fact, she prepared me for my own meeting with the Irish superstar in Toronto a few months later. When we were introduced, Bono took my hand and kissed it. He did not, however, drop to his knees as he had with Patsy. Needless to say, Bono has a knack for making backstage moms feel very special.

The downside of fame, of course, is the erosion of privacy as paparazzi and aggressive fans make normal outings difficult. Patsy likes the way Adam deals with the public and cites a recent Mother's Day event to make her point. Adam and Michael took her to see *The Book of Mormon* at a theater in LA. Adam was cordial with fans on the street, stopping for photos and shaking hands. But as she and her sons tried to work their way down the aisle to their seats, more and more people wanted a word, a handshake, a photo. Finally Adam said, "It's Mother's

New Friends

Day. I'm with my mom. But thank you so much." And she noted that everyone was understanding because he had been kind.

Not long after that, though, a publicity-seeking maniac jumped out of a throng of autograph seekers to throw something at Adam, covering his face and upper body with a white powder. The shocked pop star later learned that the substance was a harmless confectioner's-sugar "bomb," but fear from that moment remained. It could have been anything. The perpetrator, who was immediately arrested and charged with assault, had wanted his own moment in the spotlight. He had previously thrown a rock at Dwayne "The Rock" Johnson and in the incident with Adam was referencing "Sugar," the title of one of Maroon 5's new songs.

Now that Adam appears on television in *The Voice* twice a week, the intrusion of tabloid media is beginning to take a toll on Patsy, who lives simply and quietly and avoids reading or listening to gossipmongers. But friends and family call her when vicious rumors and accusations are made public to ask if they are true. Patsy is annoyed, but also sad to think that "there are hordes of fans who believe what they read."

All of the exasperations vanish when she sees Adam, now so happily married to Behati, in a relationship she believes is his "crowning achievement." She adores Behati and when I met her couldn't wait for the birth of her granddaughter. She described them all as "over the moon" about the impending arrival. And it can now be reported that Dusty Rose Levine was born in September 2016.

Patsy has retired from her admissions-counselor job, but family situations keep her busier than ever. "Time is a gift," she says as she arranges her calendar around caring for elderly parents and traveling to New York to help her stepdaughter, Julia, with her second baby. She shares her life with her husband of twenty-two years, the man she met when their children performed together in an elementary-school performance of *Joseph and the Amazing Technicolor Dreamcoat*. He enjoys acting in community theater productions and has also stepped up as the cook in the family, a task Patsy was happy to relinquish.

She's keeping a journal and hoping to join the family ranks as a writer sometime soon. An avid reader, she particularly enjoys memoirs and autobiographies and knows that her life adventures may yield some good stories. Her notebooks are full.

KELLY BRIANNE CLARKSON

Born: April 24, 1982, in Fort Worth, Texas

Kelly Clarkson (2002–present): Vocals

Genre: Pop, pop rock

First Single: "Before Your Love/A Moment Like This" (2002)

First Album: *Thankful* (2003)

JEANNIE TAYLOR

Mother of
Kelly Clarkson

IT WAS KELLY CLARKSON'S powerful voice and all-American personality that propelled her to the final rounds of the very first season of *American Idol* in 2002. Millions of television viewers voted their approval and crowned her the winner. Since then she has forged a notable career, becoming the show's most successful contestant. She has also married and had two children, all the while continuing to record, perform, tour, and win countless awards. When I met with her mother, Jeannie Taylor, in North Carolina, Kelly called from Nashville during some rare time off to make plans for a weekend family reunion. Her delighted mother was excited that she'd soon see her daughter and the adorable eight-month-old River Rose, who was giggling and gesturing on the FaceTime screen.

Life hasn't always been this pleasant for them. Jeannie Rose was born in 1951 in Belpre, Ohio, a small industrial town across the river from Parkersburg, West Virginia. The oldest of four sisters, she has few memories of her early life, she says, because of the impact of a scarring image that will not leave her memory. She remembers standing at the glass door of their tiny house, tugging at her father's legs, begging him not to leave. She was nine years old.

"He just left. We never knew why," she recalls. He moved on, marrying twice after that, working as an electrician, and for a while having his four girls visit him on weekends in the trailer home he shared with his mother. But after her junior year in high school, Jeannie never saw him again.

The small town of Belpre was confined to a three-mile area. Just over two thousand people lived there, most of them in intact families. There was one elementary school, one secondary school. There were few secrets. A scandalous affair like a father walking out would be freely gossiped about. In the late '50s school counselors and psychologists were unheard of, so hurtful glances and whispers were impossible to escape. Jeannie began to retreat into silence.

Seeing her family torn apart and her mother diminished by this abandonment made her bitter, angry, and confused. She says she felt unwanted by both parents and became a bully to her sisters. Her only solace was school, a quiet place where she knew what to do right, how to succeed. She rarely spoke. She loved to read and began the journey of what she calls "lifetime learning."

After high school she got a job in a bookstore in Parkersburg, where at twenty-one she met the man she would marry. "Head over heels in love," she embarked on the next sixteen-year chapter in her life, being a wife and mother in Fort Worth, Texas. Her first child, Jason, was born in 1973. Alyssa followed two years later, and Kelly was born in 1982.

Jeannie was busy with friends, three lively children, and a husband who was home less and less often as the years went by. When he announced that they were moving to Anaheim, California, because a new and better job awaited him, Jeannie and the kids left their house, their friends, and all they knew to join him. However, after only three months in a new house, a new city, a place where Jeannie hadn't yet had time to make new friends, her husband declared he didn't want to be married anymore. Like her mother had been, she was dumbfounded. She hadn't seen it coming. She didn't want to accept it. "I would get the kids off to school every day, then sit in a corner and cry. I couldn't do anything. I was totally devastated."

Finally Jeannie insisted on going back to Fort Worth, where she and the children had friends to help them through the difficult time. Her soon-to-be-ex-husband drove them there, dropped himself off at the airport, and said good-bye.

Much like her mother's searing memory of crying by the glass door, the image of her father leaving them at the airport so pervaded the six-year-old Kelly's mind that years later it became the setting for the song "Piece by Piece." In it she recalls watching his back as he walked away, leaving them forever. She goes on, however, to sing about a brighter future and faith restored by a man who will be kind, who will stay: her husband, Brandon Blackstock.

Brandon stood backstage with their daughter, River Rose, in his arms the night Kelly sang "Piece by Piece" for the *American Idol* final season. He watched as she was suddenly overcome with too many emotions and her tears began to flow. For the sadness of that early abandonment, for the love of her husband and daughter, for the joy of expectation of the new life she was about to birth, and for her gratitude for *Idol,* the show that had launched her career. The judges and the audience cried, too.

Kelly's mother, Jeannie, moved on and met "a good churchgoer" in Sunday school class. His strong religious views convinced her that he would be a decent father for her children. But after she married him she became aware of his erratic moods, and her children were annoyed

Early years

Cowgirl Kelly

and embarrassed by his constant sermonizing. When Kelly's friends visited, they would dart from the front door to her room to avoid the painful moralistic tirades he insisted on invoking at every opportunity. Her friends made fun of him. Alyssa couldn't stand it and moved out during her sophomore year of high school.

Kelly, who describes herself as a "creative kid with a gypsy spirit," escaped to the sanctuary of her own room to avoid the pervasive gloomy atmosphere. It was there that she could let her feelings spill out on paper. Lyrics from her song "Because of You," which Jeannie hates, reveal the hurt of the child who once again witnessed her mother's disappointment and despair and determined never to allow herself to be so diminished, to wallow in misery.

Evidently the preacher man also believed he would wait for God to bring him a job, so Jeannie had to find employment. She took a job at a before-and-after day care. She went to work early in the morning, headed from there to school to work on her degree, returned to work for the after-school day care, and then went home to care for her own children. This creative bit of planning allowed her to earn a degree in education at Texas Wesleyan, setting her up for a teaching career that would support her in the future.

After eleven difficult years, Jeannie divorced the sermonizer and took charge of her life. She taught elementary school and loved helping first graders learn how to read. She filled her summer breaks by taking even more classes, enforcing her view of a lifetime of learning that goes beyond the attainment of a degree. Even now, years after her retirement from teaching in public schools, Jeannie homeschools Alyssa's daughter every day in a specially designated area of her house.

Kelly, her mother was pleased to note, always loved to read, but most of all she loved to sing. From the age of three she was singing— in the car, or in her closet with a hairbrush microphone, or in school musicals and choirs. She didn't take voice lessons; she was a natural. People often noticed her talent and urged Jeannie to "take her somewhere" to get a career started. But Jeannie despised the image of the pushy stage mother and wanted to wait for Kelly to declare her passion for music. Besides, she wanted her to stay in school and have a normal teenage life.

I asked Kelly when she knew that music would be her future and her life's work. Her answer was surprising. "I was singing at an event at our junior high and an old man came up to me and told me singing was my purpose in life and to never stop doing it. I was thirteen and thought it amazing that a stranger would walk right up and encourage me. I thought maybe there were more strangers that would want to hear me sing, so I kept doing it!"

Jeannie describes Kelly as "a great role model, creative and independent." But there were a few problems that mother and daughter had to address during the high school years. Because she stayed up late at night filling hundreds of notebooks with lyrics and singing into the wee hours, Kelly could not force herself from her bed at the early hour her school required. Her constant tardiness resulted in a humiliating day in court for her mother, who had to face a judge's sharp question: "Do you condone this behavior?" Of course she did not, but she felt helpless to rouse the sleepy student. The court demanded that Kelly set her alarm and do community service.

After learning her lesson and mending her ways, the cheerful, optimistic Kelly reemerged and enjoyed an active school life with many friends and the various activities of a typical high school student: sports and dances and lots of music. People raved about her musical performances, which gave her the confidence to try to make a career in a very tough, selective industry. After graduating high school Kelly began auditioning for singing groups but had a difficult time. Jeannie thought that perhaps her voice was so powerful that she often overshadowed those she was singing with. She needed to be a solo artist.

Enter *American Idol*.

Kelly went to Dallas for the first audition of a show no one had heard about. The winner was promised a recording contract and the opportunity to entertain on national television, perhaps gaining fans along the way. But no one really knew what to expect. Was it just another talent show?

A grueling series of auditions moved from city to city, narrowing the group from thousands to dozens, and Kelly was able to stay in the mix. It wasn't easy. When she was expected to go to Los Angeles for the final cuts, she had no money left. Jeannie's husband refused to

With Jeannie in North Carolina

finance such a risky ploy, but the determined mother convinced the school where she taught to give her an advance in her salary, so Kelly was able to go. She could barely afford meals, but she was there. And she was winning.

Jeannie was enormously proud of Kelly's success but constantly worried about the rigorous schedule the contestants were committed to. In addition to their music preparation and performances they were shuttled from interviews and publicity events to talk shows and countless appearances. They were promoting not only themselves but this new, unproven show. Kelly called often, sometimes in tears, worried that her exhausted voice was giving out. Jeannie credits Paula Abdul, one of the show's judges, for showing concern, often bringing the young singers special teas to help soothe their overworked throats.

Kelly recalls that time as "such an intense, quick ride that everything was a challenge. Nothing I do in my entire career will compare to that first season of *American Idol*. No one was prepared for it to blow up like it did, and everyone was running around like a crazy person until that red light on the camera appeared. And then we put our best faces on to pretend that we weren't utterly exhausted and overwhelmed. It was the greatest crash course to prepare one for this industry."

When Jeannie was finally able to join the *American Idol* audience, Simon Fuller, the show's creator, told her, "Your daughter is going to be a star." Mama was proud. And Simon was right. Kelly not only won the nation's votes but went on to be the most successful contestant in the competition's history. It was just the beginning of a long, many-splendored career.

It was also the beginning of a long-awaited happy chapter in Jeannie Taylor's life. Kelly likes to have family and friends with her when she tours. Her mother has seen the world and sat at the sides of stages in Europe, Australia, Alaska, and Morocco, and has enjoyed front row seats in Las Vegas and LA, all because of her daughter's spectacular success.

In addition, Kelly's generosity has provided a lovely home for Jeannie in North Carolina, where she is just a few miles from daughter Alyssa's family. Calls from both daughters interrupted our conversation several times on the day I was there. But it was all worth it. Kelly had made a last-minute plan to send a private plane to pick up her mother and sister and fly them to Nashville for a few days. The happy grandmother would be holding her cherished River Rose very soon. And the future would hold even more blessings. In 2016 Kelly and Brandon welcomed their son, Remington Alexander Blackstock, to the world, another joyful gift in Jeannie's life.

The kindness and wisdom of the young woman who sang that "what doesn't kill you makes you stronger" has assured Jeannie that the abandonments and sad moments of the past have given way to much happier days ahead.

VIGNETTE #6

APPLAUSE!

On a cold January night in 1969 the Grohl family became a family of four. I entered the delivery room at Trumbull Memorial Hospital in Warren, Ohio, and was surprised to find a small coterie of resident physicians surrounding me. We were introduced, and the serious business of giving birth to David Eric Grohl began.

When he surfaced, there was a baby's yowl and then . . . applause! It was the first birth the new doctors had witnessed. And the first sound David Grohl heard.

As a young child David was happy, silly, goofy. He liked to make us laugh. Crazy dances, funny faces, and spot-on imitations—like his hilarious Swedish Chef—elicited the responses he so craved.

I think he was ten years old when my friend Kathleen Goldpaugh asked him to audition for a role in *Compulsion,* a dramatic play about the infamous murder in 1924 of a fourteen-year-old boy by Nathan Leopold and Richard Loeb. It would be performed at Back Alley Theater, in Washing-

ton, DC. David and another boy shared the role, performing on alternate nights, and David did quite well even if there were no laughs. He was applauded by each audience, and the director, Fred Lee, was impressed.

Several months later Fred asked David to appear in another production, this time a political roast of a US cabinet member. He would play the president's daughter, Amy Carter! Of course that meant donning a wig, dress, and patent leather Mary Janes—full juvenile drag. David instantly and resoundingly declined. But Fred persisted, offering an eighty-dollar paycheck, a kingly sum to us then.

"No thanks," David said.

"And you get a whole day out of school."

"I'm in!" was the excited response.

As I look back on the performance—that one day out of school in the ridiculous wig and navy polka-dot dress—I recall the surges of laughter and applause from the packed audience at the Sheraton Hotel. Applause moment number three.

Whatever it is about that kind of affirmation from a group I can't pretend to fully understand. I think we have to agree that it feels good to hear unanimous, loud approval for something we have accomplished. Some believe it's addictive. For a while I believed it was formative.

David left his acting career at that early age and didn't resume it until he started performing in music videos years later. The "Learn to Fly" video features David as a flamboyant airline attendant, a smitten schoolgirl (drag again!), and a pilot. Other silly, funny videos would follow.

Soon after the Amy Carter gig, David met guitar. I bought him an inexpensive acoustic instrument and a tall stool with a woven rush seat. I pictured David sitting in the kitchen strumming classical guitar music while I, glass of red wine in hand, prepared dinner.

He had an alternative vision.

Inspired by Rush, Led Zeppelin, the Beatles, and Neil Young (to name a few), he began to imitate the sounds he loved. He took a few lessons from a local teacher but much preferred his own material to the simple schoolboy tunes he was being taught, so the lessons were discontinued and he began playing with his friends in the neighborhood.

At the same time, the punk rock scene was thriving just a few miles down the road in DC and spreading its influence into the suburbs. This music was not about applause and commendation. It was about rage and dissatisfaction. It had sprung from discontent and desire for change. David embraced it, learned it, collected it . . . and began to play it. Because of his new direction I knew his music wasn't driven from the outside, from the glorious approval of a loud audience. It was so much deeper than that. The screams and rants and thundering drums weren't being played on the radio or television. They were heard in small, grungy clubs and at festivals in parks. Bands put out records a few at a time to sell at shows, and many of them went on very low-budget tours. A growing number of bands and fans in major cities across this country and in Europe proved that punk was a legitimate genre, but not one that was Grammy bound. To my knowledge there has never been a punk rock category at the Grammys, just the more palatable "alternative."

David switched to drums and played in two punk bands, starting when he was fifteen: Mission Impossible and Dain Bramage. A local entrepreneurial chap enlisted his mother to reserve the spaces, then posted flyers all over Fairfax, Arlington, and Alexandria. She and I chaperoned. The shows were fun, crowded and sweaty, but no-alcohol policies assured that they were almost, well . . . wholesome.

When David quit school to join Scream, it wasn't to get rich and famous. It was to be a part of a band and a movement that by now had ex-

cited fans in the United States and in Europe yet remained on the fringes of popular music. The applause didn't translate into dollars and could not have been called the motivating force.

I believe now that the real music makers have an unstoppable force within them that exudes melody, rhythm, lyrics, and sound. They are driven to it. They must continue to do it. And thank goodness for that! It means we still have Paul McCartney performing magnificent shows, the Rolling Stones still filling arenas, and my own beloved son writing and singing and drumming away.

Applause! Applause!

PHARRELL LANSCILO WILLIAMS

Born: April 5, 1973, in Virginia Beach, Virginia

The Neptunes, N*E*R*D (1992–present): Vocals, keyboard, drums, percussion

Genre: Hip-hop, R&B

First Album: *In My Mind* (2006)

DR. CAROLYN WILLIAMS

Mother of
Pharrell Williams

MIAMI IS WHITE-HOT the day I arrive. Gleaming glass-and-concrete condominium buildings line the beaches, blocking the water view from those outside the imposing towers. Palm trees and bright red hibiscus blossoms decorate gated entrances, where Jaguars and Porsches slide through. My Uber driver pulls up behind them, and I announce to the security guard that Dr. Carolyn Williams is expecting me.

As Carolyn strides through the lobby to greet me, I am amazed by her uncanny resemblance to her son Pharrell—the smooth gait, the straight, slim dancer-like body, the youthful face, and the broad, engaging smile. Peas in a pod!

She welcomes me, and we take the elevator to Pharrell's penthouse apartment, where she and her husband are currently staying to care for their grandson while his daddy is working in LA. They travel from their home in Virginia Beach often to guarantee lots of family time. Inside the apartment there are no walls separating us from sea and sky. Floor-to-ceiling windows circle the room where we will sit, surrounded by colorful art and scattered toys, to talk about our sons, our two boys from Virginia who might find this top-of-the-world setting an apt metaphor for their success in the music business.

We begin with the mother's story. Dr. Carolyn Williams was born and raised "down the county," as Virginia Beach folks call it. It's the farm area that surrounds Virginia's largest city. She lived with her parents, two sisters, and a brother in a house on her grandfather's farm until tragedy struck. During the annual burning of the field to prepare for spring plowing, a shift in the wind sent the flames in the wrong direction and burned to the ground everything they owned. The family had to start over, and they moved to the beach area.

Carolyn adjusted easily to the change. Just entering middle school, she became more aware of other children, more social. Her earlier years had been defined by the family circle; now she made friends easily. She loved going to school. During the unpredictable Virginia winters, I recall most kids praying for snow, keeping the radio and TV tuned to the stations that announced school closings, wishing for an extra hour of sleep and some sledding adventures on the closest hill. Not Carolyn. She says she cried when school was called off. It meant a day without the place where she felt so happy and comfortable.

It's not much of a surprise, then, to learn that Dr. Carolyn Williams has four college degrees and has spent most of her life in and around classrooms, first at Tidewater Community College, then at Old Dominion University, and next at the University of North Carolina at Chapel Hill. Her PhD is from Regent University, in Virginia Beach. She taught middle school in Virginia Beach, then accepted a librarianship and continued in that position until she retired. Her other title, Mrs. Pharoah Williams, was added when she married her life partner.

During the busy early years, Carolyn relied on her mother to help with Pharrell, the first of her three sons, each born ten years apart from the others. His high energy and humorous antics "drove her crazy," Carolyn says of her mother, and it was the harried grandmother who recommended buying him a drum because "he was always pounding away on something." This decision was the determining shift that lined up the events of Pharrell's life after that. He played in the drum line in his high school band. He organized hip-hop groups that played in and around school. Then he forged a friendship and partnership with Chad Hugo, a fellow musician he befriended at music camp. Their writing and producing collaborations won almost instant success when Teddy Riley, who had recently opened a music studio a mere block away from Princess Anne High School, where Pharrell was enrolled, heard them at a talent show and urged them to sign a contract. Riley, with Harlem roots and a long career in hip-hop and R&B, was a well-credentialed

With Carolyn in Miami

producer of Michael Jackson, Bobby Brown, Snoop Dogg, and Usher. He could spot talent when he saw it. Pharrell and friends would start off in good hands.

But Carolyn recalls those times with mixed emotions. A scholar herself, she had held high hopes for Pharrell's academic career. He was so bright, creative, energetic. "I knew he had the potential to be an A student, but he only did enough to get by, that's it, enough to get by."

Instead, he was writing beats, playing music, and spending hours at the studio. Carolyn trusted her son to stay out of trouble and spend his time well, so when he came home at midnight and said he'd been at the studio, she was fine with that. "He never gave me a reason not to trust him," she said. But his homework suffered.

Pharrell, who looks up to and admires his mother, recalls that those "complicated" times were always resolved with open communication to prevent greater problems from arising. "Mom was strict, but I appreciate it now," he says.

Carolyn began to note Pharrell's deepening commitment to musical growth. "I think the experiences he had as a child helped to create the man he became. Growing up in an environment of having to work hard, realizing that if you don't do it for yourself, you can't depend on others to do it for you," she explains. It was this framework that served as the basis for the enormous success that was to come. Pharrell had observed his parents working hard, going to school—committed to providing for a family of five—and their efforts were not lost on him.

But the music? Where did that come from, I wondered. Carolyn shakes her head as if she, too, is still wondering. They all loved music, listening to it on the radio and singing in the church choir. But there had been no family tradition of one specific type of music. Besides, the kind of music Pharrell was experimenting with didn't exist when Carolyn and Pharoah were forming their tastes. They are a religious family, so Tramaine Hawkins and the Mighty Clouds of Joy suited them just fine.

Pharrell's time in the studio and his new association with Teddy Riley proved to be productive. The rambunctious child had turned his endless energy and creativity to music he loved. "And next thing I know, we need to get an attorney to review contracts," Carolyn recalls. Her son's career was launched.

In 2004, after working with Gwen Stefani, Kanye West, Snoop Dogg, Madonna, Beyoncé, Maroon 5, Shakira, Jennifer Lopez, and Miley Cyrus, Pharrell, with his production partner Chad Hugo, won two Grammy Awards: for Producer of the Year, and for Best Pop Vocal Album for their work on Justin Timberlake's *Justified*.

Yet after all that success Pharrell still sees himself, musically speaking, as "'the help.' I kept being given opportunities to write music for people, or to perform or produce. I kept at it because it was fun."

In 2013 all "happiness" broke loose. That "Happy" song you can never get out of your head was the number-one song in the United States and twenty-two other countries. Originally written for the soundtrack of *Despicable Me 2,* and written, produced, and performed by Pharrell, it garnered seven Grammy nominations. Even the Red Army Choir recorded it! Watching the usually dour uniformed Russians do the joyous dance made me wonder . . . maybe we *can* all get along!

The rapid rise to success is a journey that causes mothers concern. But now our sons are successful, grown-up, thriving. No need to worry, right?

Wrong. Carolyn was suspicious of "the fast life—so many things that an individual could fall prey to, you have to worry." She admits that her concern never ends. She is always praying for her boys and lets them know "I'm still watching, still listening, and I don't have a problem picking up the phone. You need to hear his voice, make sure he's not tired, make sure he's taking time for himself."

Now our sons are in their forties. They have survived early hurdles and achieved huge success. We worry about their no-sleep, fast-paced lives. We used to blame their managers and their record companies for the exhausting demands, and now we realize they are making those choices for themselves. Why do they do it?

"Because they never want to disappoint," says the very wise Dr. Williams.

Pharrell's inquisitive mentality and creative enterprise have blossomed into areas of art, design, and ecology. He believes nothing is off-limits. His process of reinvention is inspired by his constant quest to find what is beyond "the box" and by asking, "How can we do this better?" He has designed apparel for his Billionaire Boys Club and Ice Cream lines. He established Bionic Yarn, an endeavor that merges environmental stewardship with fashion by turning recycled plastic into thread. He has created furniture and art that is truly original. And he's still young, not even close to being finished. Carolyn ascribes his entrepreneurial drive to the freedom he has achieved through success to "expand, to do more. There are no limitations, no boundaries" for the mind that is still searching.

Mother and son have combined their talents and their hopes for the future in a collaborative project, From One Hand to Another (FOHTA). FOHTA is a not-for-profit organization in Virginia Beach that works through schools, churches, and recreation centers to provide programs for underserved seven- to twenty-year-olds. It offers classes and camps that work to empower kids to create and learn through new technologies, art, and media. As Chairwoman of the Board and Director of Education, Carolyn oversees the burgeoning project, which now offers nine summer camps and various after-school programs for over three thousand students a year. She has written the curriculum for ThinkGreen, an ecological initiative, and established its three Rs: recycling, reusing, reducing. In addition to providing academic assistance and enhancement, the group donates school supplies, food for Thanksgiving, and toys for Christmas. Carolyn hopes to see the program expand to Miami and other cities in the near future. In an interview in an issue of *Ebony* magazine that featured him on the cover, Pharrell said, "I'm forty-one.

At this point everything I do has to be about giving back." FOHTA is just one of the ways he is achieving that.

When Pharrell was a little boy, he spent many hours in his grandmother's care while his parents worked. Now the next generation is keeping it all in the family. While Pharrell is in Los Angeles doing *The Voice* or out on tour, Carolyn and Pharoah are taking care of the youngest Williams boy, Pharrell's son, Rocket. Carolyn says history is repeating. Her inquisitive, energetic grandson is very much like his father. You instantly see the great joy and pride she and Pharoah share in caring for him. Pharoah is a wonderful man, warm and friendly—and responsible, Carolyn says, for keeping her laughing through the years. But his quiet authority is evident when he leans in to remind Rocket to be polite or to speak up. Rocket and Carolyn take piano lessons and practice together. Like his father he also loves playing drums. When they do a family trio, Pharoah joins in on bongo drums. They have not announced their next tour.

After giving me most of their day, the generous family invited me to dinner at a lovely nearby restaurant. It was there that I met Rocket and got to chat with Psolomon, the youngest of Carolyn's three sons. He, too, shares the family's quiet, friendly manner and told me of his plans to study physics. He was casually yet immaculately dressed, like someone with an eye for fashion—someone, perhaps, like his brother Pharrell.

Carolyn isn't sure where the confident fashion sense came from. Her mother was a seamstress, but not a trendsetting designer. She remembers one thing, though: the plaid shirt. When Pharrell was a boy, his teacher mom had to budget carefully to clothe her growing boys. When she noticed that a plaid shirt she had bought on sale remained at the back of his closet, unworn, she reminded him often to wear it rather than waste it. Finally he appeared one morning in plaid. But he had cut the sleeves off. And he had used that extra fabric for something—she can't quite remember what. Did he wrap it around his head? Wear it like a scarf? Whatever he did, it may have been his first fashion statement.

Years later, a large color photo appeared in the *LA Times* of Pharrell sporting his iconic hat and a plaid shirt, looking ready for *GQ*. Pharrell was described by *GQ* magazine (on whose cover he's appeared, by the way) as a "quiet little space cat of a dude" as he was photographed helping homeless children pick out the jeans and T-shirts he was giving them. I came across several such attempts to pin down his ethereal nature. The unique amalgam of spiritual groundedness, charisma, and charitable and commercial acumen seems to be a shared Williams trait. Carolyn's standard farewell is "Be blessed." She says it to everyone she encounters: the cashier at a lunch counter, the gatekeeper at her condo, guests at her home. Her radio is tuned to a religious station broadcasting a sermon in the background as we drive to lunch. Yet she radiates a joyous spirit and a sense of fun.

My meeting with Carolyn Williams took place as 2014 was coming to an end. When she spoke of Pharrell's mind-boggling impact, she didn't need to prove her claim. In that short twelve-month span his multiplatinum "Happy" continued to make us want to sing. His fashion contributions ranged from being voted Hat Person of the Year, to sporting a memorable Bermuda shorts tux, to helping save the environment by turning discarded ocean bottles into usable thread. He collaborated with Uniqlo and Adidas to design polka-dot sneakers and jackets, T-shirts, hats, and hoodies. He brought out his *Girl* album, followed by a fragrance with the same name. He continued to be the most lovable coach on *The Voice*. He appeared at Coachella and on dozens of stages and TV shows. He got a star on the Hollywood Walk of Fame. He made the *Forbes* Celebrity 100 List and *Time* magazine's list of the 100 Most Influential People in the World. Oh, and he received six more Grammy nominations.

DAVID JOHN MATTHEWS

(DAVE MATTHEWS)

Born: January 9, 1967, in Johannesburg, South Africa

Dave Matthews Band (1991–present): Lead vocals, acoustic guitar, electric guitar

Genre: Rock, folk rock, bluegrass, alternative

First Album: *Remember Two Things* (1993)

VAL MATTHEWS

Mother of Dave Matthews
(Dave Matthews Band)

"CRYSTALIZING MY LIFE," VAL MATTHEWS writes in a blog post about her move to a small house in Charlottesville, Virginia. She's describing the process of downsizing, streamlining, reorganizing all the objects that have attached to more than seventy years of life in South Africa, England, and the United States. Her life has seen sweeping political change that informed the current views of Val and her son, Dave Matthews. Her life is now quiet, less complicated, but she is still active in promoting political awareness and devoted to painting and writing poetry.

I pulled up to her modest cottage with its wide front porch and parked behind a car displaying a "Trust Women" bumper sticker. A demure, friendly woman, Val urged me inside to rooms filled with bookshelves, wildflowers in a jar atop a piano, and hospitality that made me wish I'd known her for years. We sat at an old oversized table, rescued from the downsizing, Val said, when it was clear that Christmas with her ever-growing family must continue around that table.

The late-summer sun poured through windows to reveal watercolor paintings by Val and her friends, hundreds of books bulging with yellow Post-it tabs, and an antique armoire that houses a stereo and a large collection of albums, mostly classical, but also, of course, those of the Dave Matthews Band. On the table is a Faulkner novel, and I comment that after obtaining a degree in English literature and seventy years of reading, I have declared Faulkner overrated, excusing myself from "getting him." Val laughs. She's still trying.

Val Borchers grew up in South Africa in a well-educated family. Her mother was a painter and sculptor, her father a geologist who spent his professional life as an engineer traveling to gold mines throughout South Africa. Because of her parents' frequent travels, Val went to a boarding school when she was eight and continued there until graduation. It was an English school, very strict in procedure but liberal in its teaching. There she learned to love reading and to look beyond her own safe, secure segment of society to the troubled countryside that surrounded her. She was aware from an early age of the evils of apartheid, and in her lifetime saw the radical changes that reshaped the nation of her birth.

Val's childhood was privileged; there were servants to look after the family. She recalls a boisterous kitchen where the servants, often gathered around a large table, seemed happy. Her favorite was Robert, who was with her family for as long as she can remember. She and he addressed each other as "brother" and "sister" in his language. She describes it as a relaxed, sometimes crazy, atmosphere. But to work in her family's household, the servants had to leave their families behind in the homelands or townships where they were allowed to live according to whether they were black or mixed blood.

At the University of Johannesburg, where Val was studying to be an architect, she met John Matthews. Both spent their final year of study in London and married soon after. John became a well-known electro-microscopist, a specialty in the field of molecular physics, and it was his positions as researcher and lecturer that determined their destinations. They went to New York, where he worked in an IBM laboratory; to Cambridge, England, where he spent a year at the university; and to Charlottesville, Virginia, where he was a professor at the University of Virginia. They had four well-traveled children: Peter, Anne, David, and Jane.

When the children were young, camping was a favorite activity. They headed to remote, scenic areas with one enormous tent and cooked over wood fires. Val and John enjoyed the quiet, reflective aspects of this activity, as did most of their similarly reserved children. But one of the Matthews clan, the socially adept one, often left the campfire to find new friends at adjoining campsites. That was Dave. He was always good at making friends. Looking back now, Dave admits that those forays weren't always friendly. He once saw a physical battle, a "screaming dad and his cowering, whimpering kid," and ran back to the safe confines of his family to be comforted. But the image stays with him, etched in his memory.

The social one was also the "original Quaker" in the family, Val says, drawn to the local Quaker meetings by what he thought was "a naughty group of kids" and calling it "the best fun." Val was mystified by this attraction when she began attending Quaker meetings and discovered that they consisted of long periods of silent reflection. But the Quakers were also active in antiapartheid demonstrations. Val remembers going with Dave and his Quaker pals to an ice cream parlor where the owner had prohibited blacks from sitting on the stools. The white children sat, then held their black friends in their laps. They were served, Val said, with "ill grace." Perhaps that was the "best fun" part.

That gesture of kindness is one that Val associates with her son. From an early age, she recalls, he was a kind, brave child, unafraid of standing against the crowd if he witnessed bullying or lack of fairness. She was impressed by this trait, which set him apart from so many other children. When I told Dave of his mom's compliment, he was pleased and a bit surprised. With quiet humility he responded, "I think I need to work on my opinion of myself."

Years later Dave Matthews, still unable to turn away from social injustice, would protest with his lyrics in "Cry Freedom," from the album *Crash*:

> How can I turn away
> Brother/Sister go dancing
> Through my head . . .
> Cry freedom, cry
> From a crowd ten thousand wide
> Hope laid upon hope
> That this crowd will not subside

John Matthews's untimely death from cancer left Val a young widow with four children who were eight, ten, twelve, and fourteen. She

Poems about This and That
By Val Matthews

Val Matthews, poet

remembers their surprising sensitivity to her grief during that time. If she snapped at one of them, they all rallied round, making her comfortable with a moment or two of rest, a glass of sherry, and a bit of classical music on the stereo. They were caring and protective, reflecting the strong family unit that Val and John had created.

Although Dave was only ten he knew how much he would miss his father. A memory he says is now tattooed on his mind recalls early struggles to climb into his father's lap and the feeling of those strong hands supporting him under his arms, launching him to that safe, comforting spot.

It was difficult raising four children alone, and Val wasn't sure where she should be, in the United States or South Africa. She tried both. When she took her children back to her home country, much had changed. Apartheid was replaced by confusion and turmoil during the difficult transition period. Barred windows and fences had provided security before, but now security was tightened. And there were guns, one of the new freedoms. Val's niece was traumatized by a carjacking incident in which her car and wedding ring were stolen by a gun-wielding thug. Folks were nervous. Confusion reigned.

Val told her children that when they returned to South Africa they would look after themselves without a household staff, just as they had in America. But women looking for jobs lined up outside her house, and she eventually hired one of them. Thinking you were showing solidarity with black South Africans by doing your own work was not the reality. Laws had been changed, but sadly a perfect society was still a hopeful dream. People needed to be educated and trained for the jobs they were now allowed to hold, and a great deal of corruption followed the reorganization of power. Val says it was very sad to see all those hopes met with such disappointment.

The Matthews children were schooled in both the South African and American systems, neither of which held much appeal for Dave. A bright, artistic child, he brought home report cards that often reflected his lack of interest and effort. At one unforgettable private-school conference, Val remembers a teacher asking Dave what he did on weekends. "I do my music and my art," he replied.

"And where do you think that's going to get you?" the clueless teacher retorted.

Val fairly simmers as she tells the story. She and I have both been through this territory many times. It is hard to forgive school programs that can't find ways to generate interest from kids who show great talent and commitment to artistic endeavors. It is my profound hope that someday, somehow, our school systems will begin to reflect the diversity of their student population. Much attention, or at least speech-making, has addressed the need for cultural and racial diversity. But that's just a small part of the need for change. We must find a way to involve the creative minds of those artists and thinkers who don't always move comfortably according to the patterns our schools set up. It may be that we need to rethink the hiring and training of teachers to allow a few creative minds into those ranks. As for administrators, I remain pessimistic. But an easy first step might be for them to actually visit a classroom. In over thirty years in those classrooms, I saw them only when I invited them, and they always seemed surprised that I did so.

Dave remembers watching Val at work on her paintings, many of which he still has. She encouraged him to draw and paint as well. He loved making art, considering it "a pleasurable way to exhaust the hours." He still appreciates how supportive she was of his love for art and music. Although he resisted taking art and music classes, he continued to pursue those endeavors on his own. And now he is known for both. His paintings and designs grace his album covers, and, of course, his poetry is the backbone of his music.

Dave finished high school somehow and decided to return to the United States, spending some time in New York and then moving to

Charlottesville, Virginia, where Val and the other family members later joined him. Before the children were born, Val and John had spent a few years in Charlottesville when John was a professor at the University of Virginia. Val had had little enthusiasm for moving to the States, considering America a place where everyone had "perfect teeth, new cars . . . and guns." But she grew to like Charlottesville, and it became, so many years later, her place of choice when she "crystalized and downsized."

Tucked in the foothills of the magnificent Blue Ridge Mountains and surrounded by rolling hills of farms, orchards, and wineries, Charlottesville is a city of around fifty thousand people. The tradition of Thomas Jefferson, the area's most famous son, can be seen in the neoclassical architecture at the university and at Jefferson's home, Monticello. But within the city one senses a unique confluence of vibrant intellectual, cultural, and artistic elements. Artists of all types choose Charlottesville because they can be close to other artists and part of an ever-changing slate of art and music shows in a friendly, nonintimidating haven. It was exactly the right place for the young Dave Matthews, who arrived without clear intent or a determined destination. It was a place where he could hear music every night or experiment with one or two other musicians. In Charlottesville you are always a block or two away from other music makers. You go to the same shows at the few clubs that book them. But you also have a regularly revolving audience because the UVA student population of twenty thousand changes every year. The arts environment there is a unique melting pot.

Dave appreciated the fact that the Charlottesville scene allowed him to cross barriers that would have been more formidable in other places. He could play rock music with a saxophonist and a fiddle player. He didn't have to "choose sides," he said, and his "curiosity about music and art could be indulged." The Dave Matthews Band began with a singer and the songs he had been writing for a year in his mother's basement. He began inviting musicians whose prowess he admired to experiment with him. His first two members were a jazz drummer and a sax player. Later a keyboard player and violinist were added. This unique combination yielded some startling sounds, and it took a while for things to come together. According to their own reports, the first attempts were horrible.

Val's basement continued to be the practice space for the band. She didn't comment on their sound, but she worried that her elderly neighbors would object to the loud, late-night sessions as the full volume of the music filled the neighborhood. When a neighbor called, asking to see Dave, they feared the worst. But Mrs. Hankins, in a lovely gesture of Southern hospitality, had baked sugar buns for the band. She felt safe, she said, having all those nice young men so close by.

Val and I laughed at that bit of good luck, and I told her how I never had the problem of noisy rehearsals because my house was always the smallest and had no basement. But when I moved to California, karma got me. Just inches from my patio wall sat a drum kit, where an aspiring musician and his friends gathered regularly. Now I know.

The band used Val's beat-up white station wagon to get to its gigs. In the early days the gigs were in Charlottesville and Richmond and surrounding areas. My daughter, Lisa, remembers going to the band's shows on the Outer Banks of North Carolina in tiny, crowded clubs, where fans loved this new, hard-to-classify music.

Nowadays the old wagon has been replaced by tour buses, and the tiny, sweaty clubs by huge arenas and festival venues. Val has been in attendance, but in her humorously self-deprecating fashion she describes herself as "awfully irritable." Having been given a good seat, she doesn't understand why everyone must stand up and ruin her view. And she is annoyed that the audience sings. She would prefer to see and hear

At home with Val

the band. So now, she says, they give her a little supply of airplane-size scotch bottles and find her an out-of-the-way, safe place, and the show goes on. When you meet this very charming, quiet woman, you know this is a great joke that she likes to tell on herself.

Val's music of choice has always been classical. In earlier days Dave was jolted from his bed by blasts of full-volume Bach, his mother's foolproof method for getting four children awake and ready for school. Music played at a less punishing volume surrounded them the rest of the time. Classical music was an integral part of life in the Matthews house. Val described her mystical response to certain sounds, the "pure emotional connection" to music that many of us feel. She spoke of drumrolls and surges in music that make her cry for no apparent reason. She also told of the emotional hold John Lennon's "Imagine" had on her and her son when they listened to it together and cried, moved by the song's poetry and music.

Val has been writing poetry for years and is quite proud of her son's poetic lyrics. She describes her own work as moments condensed, the "whipped cream" moments that one endeavors to save. Her poetry fills books that she gives to her grandchildren, wonderful keepsakes of vignettes she has penned, a "record of [her] life," she says. Here's one of them:

SUNRISE IN BELMONT
The sun rises up from behind the little mountain,
Sometimes a flaming red circle, sometimes gold.
It puts the trucks and tanks and stores in a deep shade,
And then its rays beam right through my little house,
Lighting up the piano on the far wall;
Showing up all the dust and hair and grass
Shed inside;
Showing up the grandchildren's finger marks
And dogs' nose marks on the glass doors.
But briefly, there is a magic brilliance
In my house and in my life.

There seems to be a tradition in Val's family to record the daily aspects of life, the everyday things that some call mundane but that have value upon examination, especially when we lose them. After Val's father wrote his memoirs, he told her the process of recalling his life was like pulling the end of a ball of string. More and more came out as he pulled, memory piled on memory. Now Val writes about the family's relationship with their mailman in "A Postal Lament," a charming essay about the times when the mailman would stop to chat and help with an unwieldy package. The underlying significance is the sad realization that this is a story of the past.

Dave, also a close observer of events around him, writes prolifically of personal lives, of injustices large and small; yet, like Val, he sounds almost cheerful as his pleasing, lilting melodies repeat. He sounds hopeful.

These days, when she isn't writing poetry or doing sketches and watercolors, Val is busy with a myriad of important activities. She regularly helps children with reading at the nearby elementary school. She takes care of grandchildren in her toy-filled sunroom. And she stays current with important issues and concerns by reading what she calls "depressing books" that explore social movements and history. She doesn't have a television set.

Recently Dave was chosen to give the opening remarks at the yearly citizenship ceremony held at Monticello. Val sat in the first row, undisturbed now by rude fans and filled with pride as her youngest son bestowed the honors on the local new citizens. It was a fitting venue and a fitting event for these two remarkable citizens of the world, Dave and Val Matthews.

VIGNETTE #7

NIRVANA

Today I opened a box of memories, a carton of saved memorabilia from David's Nirvana years. Flooded with nostalgia and stung again with the painful recall that surrounds that time, I read some of the *Rolling Stone* and *Spin* articles from 1992. It was hard. "Nirvana is on a collision course with the world," Lauren Spencer opined in *Spin*. She could not have known how prophetic her words would prove to be.

Just two years before that article was published, my son had landed in Seattle, Washington. Scream, the band he had dropped out of school to tour with, had completed a successful tour of Europe, then limped across the United States, making enough money in Pittsburgh to get to Cleveland, and enough there to get to Detroit, and so on. They were surviving. Barely. But when the bass player was no longer available (I believe he took his talents to a county jail), they were broke and stuck in LA. I had no idea how desperate the situation was. There were no anguished calls or pleas for money or a plane ticket. David kept in touch, but he always sounded like the cheerful, upbeat son who had left, feeding my blissful oblivion.

His desperation ended when he was drafted by a new band that was in search of their fifth drummer. My obliviousness continued as David moved into a squalid apartment with Kurt Cobain and learned the music of his new band, Nirvana. His calls were still uncomplaining. He was on the other side of the country with no money and no friends, but on the phone he seemed only upset about the cold, rainy weather. The full story unfolded years later.

Enter now the chorus of practical, realistic parents. *You never should have let him go. He was too young. I could have told you this would happen.*

The fact is, things changed quickly. David's drum sound was a good fit. Nirvana played shows in Olympia and Seattle, and people noticed. Within six months of David's arrival the band signed with a major label and were sent to Sound City Studio in LA to record what would become a chart-

Nirvana,
Krist Novoselic, Kurt Cobain & Dave Grohl

shaking album, *Nevermind*. They replaced Michael Jackson as number one on the *Billboard* 200 a few months later, toured the world playing in huge arenas, and were recognized everywhere they went. They were as shocked and surprised at their celebrity as any of the chorus of naysayers. This kind of fame and fortune hadn't been part of the plan.

Enter the press. TV, newspapers, magazines. All of them. All the time. Everywhere.

Krist Novoselic, the six-foot-seven bassist with a formidable intelligence and a weird sense of humor, tried to keep the press at bay by mystifying them. Kurt, his best friend, retreated to corners or behind doors or appeared angry, surly, unapproachable. And David, who referred to himself as "just the drummer," tried valiantly to be true to himself, which meant to be kind and funny, to be entertaining. In Lauren Spencer's article she referred to Kurt as "possibly tormented" and to David as "seriously fun."

Lisa and I headed west for our first California trip to see several shows featuring Nirvana, the Red Hot Chili Peppers, and Pearl Jam, an all-star lineup. The 1991 New Year's Eve show in San Francisco was one we'll remember forever, with an arena full of revelers and three of the decade's best bands giving their all. I was introduced to the youthful crew that worked ardently and joyously behind the scenes to make sure the sound, lights, stage, and instruments were perfect. I met the managers and accountants, radio people, record company people—*so many people*! This was no longer a little three-piece band playing on a small stage in a seedy club. This was the big time.

The bleak days when the kids go from city to city with just enough money for hot dogs and Slurpees aren't what mothers of the musician-adventurers fear. It's that next step, the one where money and fame replace impoverished obscurity. What will all that money be used for? What and who will enter the picture once fame is the new reality?

Geddy Lee's mother, Mary, had thought about that and was terrified from the beginning about drugs. She knew they were out there and that they were often associated with rock bands. The stories were never happy ones. Geddy promised her he would never let her down. Verna Griffin, Dr. Dre's mother, had already worked her way through the dangerous realities of the Compton culture and certainly knew that people would be coming at her son from all angles. There must have been many sleepless nights for Verna. We had all heard about "sex and drugs and rock and roll." Was it true? I knew about all the pot smoking. That wasn't alarming. Most of my high school students (and, if truth be told, quite a few of their teachers) were doing that. But David had vowed he would never use cocaine or heroin. I believed him.

"Really?" said the not-so-silent majority. "That's what they all say. Classic denial."

Yes. Really.

Then the story unfolded in short, tragic chapters. Fans were drawn to Kurt's rebellion and alienation. They admired the rebel who wouldn't show up for interviews, who turned into a mysterious recluse. As the gold and platinum records piled up, his will deteriorated. Overdoses and canceled shows and tours replaced the thrilling firsts of big festivals that drew thousands of fans. Lawsuits and publishing battles replaced reports of new projects and tours. Three short, dramatic years—that was all. In the end, one gunshot.

Searing pain. Irreversible loss. The music stopped.

Left in this wake of misery were Kurt's mother, wife, daughter, and two bandmates. All bereft, but still hounded by the ever-hungry press who hoped to record their anguish. Most of them were rendered speechless by the power of that loss.

Eventually, of course, life resumed. It had to. The saddened survivors set out in different directions. There will never be the right words to translate those three amazing years into a narrative that makes sense to a reader, even to the players in the drama after the curtain had come down.

For David there was a long, stunned silence. But the music finally returned. When it did, he was no longer the boy who was "just the drummer." He was a young man who would make much more music and reach far beyond the expectations of those turbulent years. He would become husband, father, producer, director, singer, composer, documentary filmmaker, and friend. He would find a much more blissful nirvana.

I'll put the lid back on my carton of memorabilia now. I'm glad there are three cartons next to it. They hold happier stories.

ZAC BROWN

Born: July 31, 1978, in Atlanta, Georgia

Zac Brown Band (2003–present): Lead vocals, guitar, banjo, bass guitar

Genre: Country

First Single: "Chicken Fried" (2003)

First Album: *Home Grown* (2005)

BETTYE MOSES

Mother of Zac Brown
(Zac Brown Band)

SURROUNDED BY MILES OF OPEN FIELDS and a few patches of wooded areas, the large red-brick retirement community stands alone. It looks new, neat, quiet. There's an elderly woman smoking a cigarette on a patio chair, but no one else in sight. I had driven here from Atlanta to talk to Zac Brown's mother, Bettye Moses. Early research told me that he was one of nine children and had a brother nineteen years his senior, so I was expecting a short interview and wanted to arrive before Bettye needed some rest, before a caretaker might interrupt us.

A vivacious woman greeted me at the door and immediately introduced me to several residents in the lobby. She pointed out the modern lounge area and the bistro where breakfast is provided. "And the people here are great," she said, her blond curls bouncing, as she whisked me down the hall to the elevator. "This is just a fun, easy place to be!" She was turning the key in the door of an apartment that I was certain she was about to sell me when I interrupted. "Excuse me, but I'm here to meet Bettye Moses."

A short pause. Then, "Oh, my! I should have introduced myself. . . . I just assumed. . . . I'm Bettye!"

I had assumed that Bettye Moses would be in her eighties, perhaps using a walker or wheelchair (after all those children!). The high-energy, youthful Southern Belle took me by surprise.

Bettye and I laughed about our awkward start for the rest of the afternoon. She's not what one expects to find in a "retirement apartment."

Not what one expects the mother of a large brood, one of whom is almost sixty, to look like.

Elizabeth Clanton (now Bettye) grew up in Smyrna, Georgia, the youngest of three sisters. When she was ten, her mother went to work in a department store. The two older sisters were fifteen and twenty-three, so Bettye learned to be independent at an early age. She had to fend for herself. As she was preparing to graduate from high school in 1966, her father was in his seventies and in poor health. She needed college funds, so she began entering pageants and beauty contests. She was a contestant in the Miss Dogwood Festival, crowned Miss AIR (Atlanta International Raceway), and sang "Moon River" in another pageant, for which she won $2,600. She saved enough to go to Memphis State, where she spent the next four years. The student revolutions and marches of the '60s held no interest for Bettye. She wanted to work, to study business, and to figure out how to make money without wasting time.

After graduation and gaining experience in a number of jobs, Bettye returned to Atlanta and started her own company selling coated paper, a specialized product necessary for the growing business-machines industry. She hired a few friends and began canvassing the city. Along the way she met Jim Curry, who was the purchasing agent for Georgia Institute of Technology. He became the first of her three husbands. Theirs was a short two-year marriage, but the best part of the union was the birth of her first child, Malcolm. Though soon single again, she was still young, energetic, and ambitious.

Next, Bettye went to work in sales and marketing for a publishing company. She was the first woman to have a baby seat in her company car. She and Malcolm made the rounds together.

As a child Bettye had enjoyed hunting and fishing and one weekend went on a dove-hunting trip with friends. It was there that she met Jim Brown, "the most charming person I've ever known in my life." Although he was thirteen years older and divorced with three children (nineteen, fifteen, and nine), it was a whirlwind romance. They married and three years later added their own son, Zac, to the suddenly large family of seven as he and Malcolm joined Jim's Wynn, Jodi, and Meredith. And Bettye was still in her twenties!

Bettye worked with Jim in his Atlanta insurance business until Zac was born. Her voice softens and she smiles broadly when she recalls that "he was the happiest baby I think I've ever seen. All he did was laugh." She adds that he was also very loud and incredibly energetic. She, Jim, and her boys settled into a house on Lake Lanier, a scenic recreation area just outside Dahlonega, Georgia. It was her dream home. Even though her marriage to Jim did not thrive, she stayed there for many years.

Zac credits his mother with introducing him to the songs of James Taylor, Jim Croce, and others. When he was seven, she arranged for weekly classical guitar lessons and later added voice lessons. In an area known for a variety of musical genres—including bluegrass, country, and mountain music—Zac was establishing an uncharacteristically broad repertoire of music, both classical and country, something that clearly defines his music today. Thanks, Mom!

Bettye, who describes herself as an eternal optimist, got married again, to Jody Moses, a successful local dentist with two young daughters. "I thought we were going to be the Brady Bunch," she says. Jim had recently found a new wife as well. He and Harriette, who also had two daughters, were not far away, so Zac was able to spend every other weekend with them.

Bettye and Jody were married for twenty-two complicated years. At one point Malcolm left to move back to his father's house. Zac did, too. "As soon as I could legally leave, I did," he told me. The legal age in Georgia was fourteen. He left the tension-filled atmosphere of Bettye and Jody's house to go live for about a year with Jim and Harriette—until Jim had to move to Atlanta for his job. With just one year of school left, Zac wanted to stay in Dahlonega, so Jim rented him an apartment above the garage of a friend of Zac's, Daniel Meeks, so that Zac could attend his senior year in high school while living independently. Zac is still grateful for the dinners the Meekses and other families cooked for him and for his Christian faith for keeping him "solid" during that time.

Dahlonega, Georgia, where Jim Brown had settled by the Chestatee River, is a small town at the base of the mountains in North Georgia. Coffee shops, guitar shops, and small music venues can be found on several of the streets that surround the classic old brick courthouse in

With Bettye...
at Camp Southern
Ground

the town's central square. The old building now houses the Dahlonega Gold Museum, where the story of the first gold rush in the United States, which occurred in 1828, is told. The area also boasts a number of wineries, so wine shops with tasting rooms can be found among the charming little storefronts. The picturesque surrounding contryside is a sportsman's mecca as well.

The town was Zac's playground. When he wasn't in school he could listen to music, play on the street, or book his own gigs in the coffee shops and music venues. He could play covers or try out his own songs. During his seminal year of independence, he learned how to take care of himself. He also learned how to be an entertainer.

When Zac looks back at the periods of separation from his mother, he expresses no bitterness. He recalls an affectionate, loving woman who tried very hard to assure that there would be financial security even as other aspects of stability eluded her family. He speaks of her "superhuman compassion" and believes that his songwriting reflects that. He said that writing about conflict has led to a deeper understanding of the various hands we're all dealt. His own compassion has allowed him to accept and forgive.

When Bettye and Jody finally divorced, she sold the Lake Lanier home she had loved so much and escaped to the Florida Keys, where she and Jody had bought a house ten years earlier. Amid the turquoise waters of her "paradise," she was able to breathe the tropical air and relax in a suddenly quiet world. But Bettye doesn't sit still for long. She moved to Charleston, bought a house, and, ever entrepreneurial, set up a new business. That was her last stop before moving to the cozy Atlanta-area apartment where we're now trading stories and looking at old photos of her mother and sisters and more recent ones of grandkids in sports uniforms.

Before I leave she drives me out to the area being developed for Zac's most ambitious project, Camp Southern Ground. When Bettye enrolled Zac in a camp many years ago, she had no idea how it would change his life, how his time spent as a camper and counselor would lead him to dedicate his life to this endeavor, this "four hundred fifty acres of magic," as Zac calls it.

When I spoke to Zac in the spring of 2016, he said that the camp had operated for four weeks the previous summer and would be open for six in 2016. The goal is for it to operate year round—not just as a camp for all children, including many with special needs, but as a research facility and an organic farm. A broad range of activities will provide future campers with unforgettable experiences in music, aquatics, nature appreciation, technology, and counseling. It is a far-reaching, very brave, and extraordinarily expensive project. Seeing the area in person was wonderful, but viewing the website, which includes a site plan illustrating the camp's planned expansion, is exhilarating.

As my afternoon with Bettye came to an end, I was more convinced than ever that the things mothers are most proud of are the magnanimous efforts our sons and daughters make that reach far beyond their music and their fame. Zac and Bettye's story is an affirmation of that.

Born: July 31, 1978, in Atlanta, Georgia

Zac Brown Band (2003–present): Lead vocals, guitar, banjo, bass guitar

Genre: Country

First Single: "Chicken Fried" (2003)

First Album: *Home Grown* (2005)

HARRIETTE BROWN

Stepmother of Zac Brown
(Zac Brown Band)

WHEN ZAC BROWN GAVE ME permission to include his mother in my book project, he insisted that I meet two women: his birth mother, Bettye, and his stepmother, Harriette Brown. No explanation was given, but by the end of my day in Senoia, Georgia, I began to understand why my meeting Harriette had been important to him.

Harriette had invited me to meet her at Zac's restaurant in Senoia (say SEN-NOY, please; drop the *A* at the end), a small town that is so charming and beautiful I'm surprised I had never heard of it. It's been there, all five square miles of it, since 1860, when it was known as a rich agricultural area. More than one hundred exquisitely restored houses listed on the National Register of Historic Places sit side by side a block or two away from the commercial area. The houses exhibit Queen Anne, Gothic, and Victorian styles and are decorated with wraparound porches, gables, and turrets. A half-hour drive around the town introduces a visitor to these treasures, all built between 1860 and 1890 and yet so beautifully tended they look brand new. It's not surprising to learn that many Southern-themed films have been shot there, including *Fried Green Tomatoes* and *Driving Miss Daisy*. Currently the television series *The Walking Dead* is filmed there.

The three-block commercial area consists of small shops, bakeries, boutiques, cafes, and museums lining both sides of a boulevard. Brick sidewalks lead visitors to restored tin-roofed buildings, where canvas awnings cover doors and windows that have been there for a hundred years. I haven't seen a town this picturesque since I toured the Cotswolds in England. One of the signs announces Southern Ground restaurant, and Harriette is approaching just as I walk up.

First she shows me around. Zac has long loved to cook, and this is his second restaurant. It looks like an old-fashioned saloon, with a gleaming bar at the back, a long row of booths on one side, dartboards on the wall, and a skeleton seated at a piano in the corner. Posters announce live music and special events. There's a friendly vibe, a sort of "where everybody knows your name" feel about the place. As we entered it was filling with lunch patrons.

I was treated to fried green tomatoes, meatballs, and more—plate after plate of delicious Southern fare. Harriette wanted me to sample everything. As I did, she told me her story.

Harriette was born and raised in Hogansville, Georgia, another small town not far from Senoia. She was the youngest of five, but separated from her siblings by a wide age gap. When she was in third grade, the sibling closest to her age graduated from high school. Sometimes it seemed like she was an only child.

Life was simple in that small town in the '50s. Nobody locked doors, car keys were left in the car, and children roamed freely. There was safety in knowing everyone in town.

"I grew up in a Christian home. God came first and I knew it. My parents were married fifty-four years, and my daddy adored my mama. She was five feet two, a little bit of a thing who had me at noon on Sunday in the doctor's office and was home making biscuits at four o'clock!"

Harriette's father worked for a textile company for many years but upon retirement became a minister in the Primitive Baptist church. She grew up "at the church every time the doors were open and loved it. Still do, you know?" She sang in the church choir, always a cappella because the Primitive Baptists don't allow musical instruments to be played inside their churches. Fortunately for Zac it seems they were OK outside the church doors.

Harriette played French horn in her school band and developed an early love of the energetic dance known as the Shag. She began competing in shag-dancing contests quite early and enjoyed performing it for

Brown family pajama party

Young Zac

years. She passed the dance gene to her daughter, who won several national championships years later.

In the sixth grade Harriette began "going with" Harold, her steady boyfriend all through school. After graduation from high school she got a job in Atlanta working for *Parents* magazine as the regional director's assistant. Harold was drafted and sent to Vietnam. They became engaged shortly before he deployed and were married nine days after he returned.

"But a lot had changed," she mused as she thought back to those difficult years in the '60s when the world seemed suddenly less predictable. They had two girls, Allison and Kelly, but divorced after twelve years of marriage. About a year later Harold married Barbara, whom Harriette refers to as her "wife-in-law."

When her daughters were spending weekends with their father and Barbara, Harriette sensed that they felt guilty about leaving their mother and disloyal if they showed affection for Daddy's new wife. Knowing that Barbara was a kind woman and always good to her girls, Harriette counseled them to "love whoever is good to you and loves you. Don't worry about hurting my feelings." It's no surprise, then, that although Harold died fifteen years ago, Harriette and Barbara are still close friends.

Harriette remained single for five years. Then she met Jim Brown. She was thirty-nine, he was fifty, and the story sounded to me like the classic "love at first sight." She knew that he was divorced and had a few children. Their first date didn't go well. Harriette's job, with the owner of the Ritz-Carlton in Atlanta, meant she often had access to tickets for Atlanta Falcons football games. When she invited Jim to join her, he said he'd bring his youngest son along. That's when she learned that Zac was only five years old and not the least bit impressed by Falcons tickets. The afternoon was less than a success.

Zac spent his weekdays with his mother and stepfather and couldn't wait for weekends with his dad, his best pal. He and Jim were inseparable outdoorsmen, hunting and fishing buddies. When Zac was eighteen months old his father converted a cooler into a makeshift stroller and took him on his first hunting trip. Zac killed and cleaned his first deer when he was eight. They are best friends to this day. Jim travels all over the world with Zac, taking a fishing pole along in hopes that a day off will give them some good-old father-son time.

When Harriette married Jim two years later, she took on the role of taskmaster. She felt cheated as a child that her mother had never taught her to take care of herself—to cook, do laundry, keep house. She would not let that happen in her own household. She explained to Jim that breaking all the strict rules that Bettye and Jody required during the week was confusing to a child; allowing late bedtimes and no structure when Zac visited them was not a good idea. Harriette knew she would not be popular with Zac for a while but held firm. She made demands about house chores. She recalls that when Zac moved in with them full-time at twelve he was used to having his mother pick up his clothes and do his laundry. Not in Harriette's house! As soon as her girls could reach the washer and dryer they were responsible for their own clothes. So when Zac moved in he was greeted with the orders of the day.

"OK, you clean your room, you wash and dry your clothes, you clean your bathroom, take out the trash, and feed the dog." Amen. And he did. Harriette doesn't sugarcoat the early stages of their relationship. It wasn't easy at first, but they worked it out and became close.

Zac was a born musician. At first he sang with his father, who played the guitar, and with his much older brothers. His lessons began when he was seven, and the first recital occurred when he was eight. Harriette remembers that day. She recalls the intensity of his connection to music and of the talent he clearly displayed. She watched him play for hours at home, and she knew he took his guitar to school and played during lunch and recess.

Harriette continued to be impressed with Zac's recitals and performances, but as a sports fan she was really excited to see Zac and his friend Radford, both fourteen, sing the national anthem at an Atlanta Braves game. She had witnessed their rehearsals at home and nervously watched as they filled the stadium with their song. She thought it was perfect.

She was not so pleased at another, later performance. A teenage Zac played wherever he could get a gig and was invited to perform a fifteen-minute opening set in a club near Harriette's work. She invited people from her office to join her to see the son she so often bragged about. Zac knew to be careful when he played a show with Harriette in attendance. He tried to be respectful of her strong religious views, tried to avoid unsavory topics or "dirty words." Often he would put questionable songs at the end of a set list when he knew Harriette would have left. But this night he had only fifteen minutes. And he was going to play "The Devil Went Down to Georgia."

"It's a great song," Harriette said. "Just don't say son-of-a-bitch." But in the heat of the performance of the up-tempo song, it slipped out. When Zac saw Harriette's shocked expression, he apologized. "I swear, it just came out!"

She laughs about it now. She has mellowed a bit and tries to keep her mind on catchy tunes and great rhythms and to not stress out about a few lyrics.

Zac got a voice scholarship to college but changed his major to business when the music-school rules prevented him from continuing with his band activities, a bit of ironic overadministrating. Later he decided to stop school altogether, to put all his efforts into building a band and a future. Harriette and Jim were fully supportive, thinking that he could always go back to school if his musical endeavors didn't work out. Bettye and Jody strongly disagreed. But none of their arguments meant much to the determined singer, songwriter, and guitar player who was about to be a star. He was ready to go for it.

Harriette tells me about each member of the Zac Brown Band, lauding their talents. She knows all their backgrounds, all the contributions each makes individually. It is a masterful group. Their music crosses genres and often defies description. (I once labeled a performance they did with David as "bluegrass grunge.") It's just great music.

A memorable moment, a highlight for Harriette, occurred on a Thanksgiving Day some time ago. After dinner, Zac asked Harriette and Jim to come out to his car, where he slid a CD into the stereo and they heard "Chicken Fried" for the first time. He wondered if they liked it. Liked it? They loved it! Harriette predicted it would be his first number-one song. Bettye had a similar story. Zac called her at two in the morning to ask her to listen on the phone to his new song. She, too, knew this was the one. They were both right. Soon it was all over the radio. Harriette loved flipping from station to station to hear how many were playing it at one time. She was so proud of him!

Lunch at Southern Ground with Harriette

After playing all those street corners and tiny clubs, and enduring stops and starts in his career, Zac Brown is now known the world over. His band plays sold-out concerts at Madison Square Garden and Wrigley Field and performs at festivals that bring in fifty to a hundred thousand fans. They appear on TV and book tours in Australia, England, Ireland, and other countries. In the past six years they have earned over fifty-five nominations from the Grammys, the Country Music Association, and many more. The fiercely independent young man who has had a guitar in his hands for over thirty years also operates his own Southern Ground Studio, in Nashville, and keeps a full schedule of producing, recording, writing, and performing.

Bettye, Harriette, and I have shared some proud moments. The first was at the 2013 CMA awards, which were broadcast on television, when my David played drums for their Zac and astounded a shrieking crowd of country and rock fans. They sang and played together at the Veterans Day Concert for Valor, on the grounds of the US Capitol. And they played together on David Letterman's show to preview the *Sonic Highways* segment on Nashville that featured a long, introspective conversation between David and Zac about mavericks in the music industry.

Harriette and Jim Brown have been married for twenty-nine years, and she still calls him "Mr. Wonderful." She tries to keep up with fifteen grandchildren near and far. She hates to fly, so she stays home when Jim travels with Zac, but she has a mountain retreat, a little cottage with a front porch, where she can escape the torrid Georgia summer heat. She can travel there by car.

I met Jim at their log cabin house at the end of our afternoon in Senoia and found him to be as advertised: charming and wonderful. As I drove away through the woods that surround their lovely home, a deer scampered across the lawn. I really hated to leave that peaceful scene and the magical little town. I'll have Georgia on my mind for a long time. If I do travel back there, I'll have to forego the fried green tomatoes at Southern Ground. The restaurant closed last year when Zac introduced his latest venture, Z Alexander Brown Wines, and became aware of an obscure Georgia law (called a Tide law) that prohibits anyone who owns more than 5 percent of a spirits company from having a liquor license.

But perhaps I will see Zac sitting on his porch with a glass of cabernet sauvignon. He'll pick up his guitar and sing his iconic song "Chicken
Fried." I'll dish up a bit of it for y'all:

> You know I like my chicken fried
> And cold beer on a Friday night
> A pair of jeans that fit just right
> And the radio on
>
> And my house it's not much to talk about
> But it's filled with love that's grown in Southern Ground
>
> I like to see the sun rise
> See the love in a woman's eyes
> Feel the touch of a precious child
> And know a mother's love.

It's just like he told me: "I love my mom and my stepmom very
much. They both taught me different things, and they both deserve to
be honored for making my life meaningful. I'm very thankful."

VIGNETTE #8

9/11

Sirens screamed outside my window, a constant cacophony of speeding emergency vehicles that extended from the Pentagon to my usually quiet suburban Virginia neighborhood ten miles away. For several hours the television screen replayed the horrors of that morning, September 11, 2001, and again and again I watched the Twin Towers collapse and the Pentagon cave in. What was happening? What was next?

My son and daughter were in California listening to the same dire reports, fully aware that the house they had grown up in was minutes away from the Pentagon disaster. Their first call to me was an urgent request for me to leave Virginia right away. By then, of course, the sky had been cleared of all flights nationwide and would remain so indefinitely. My best option was to drive cross-country to reach them, about twenty-three hundred miles.

I tried to enlist a friend to accompany me, but her responsibilities would keep her in Virginia. I reported back to California command central and assured my nervous children that I would be safe, that I wasn't panicked or fearful, that I'd call every day.

A short time later David called back. "Mom, can you be ready in two hours? I've found a tour bus."

So I arranged for a house- and cat-sitter, threw mismatched shoes, a toothbrush, and a few days' worth of clothing into a bag, and sat by the window to wait.

The enormous tour bus filled my little cul-de-sac. I could see neighbors at their windows wondering what the Grohl family was up to this time. I hadn't had time to call anyone to explain. The bus driver, who had just traveled up from North Carolina, came to the door, introduced himself as Barney, and carried my bag to the bus, where the only other passenger, the manager of Gov't Mule, sat waiting.

We got on the highway and headed east. We were driving to the outskirts of New York City, where the final passenger, Warren Haynes, would

With my 9/11 busmates Warren Haynes
and Matt Busch

board. Warren is the singer and genius guitarist of Gov't Mule and was intent on getting to Denver for a gig in two days.

So began our strange journey. Four disparate souls, confused by the chaotic events of the day, driving out of harm's way to further uncertainty. The changing landscape outside the bus windows was inspirational. American flags flew from cars, high poles, and porches. In Indiana miles of flat, barren fields yielded the most astonishing image, an enormous bright-green John Deere tractor working a field with a large American flag billowing behind.

We told stories to pass the time—of the places we'd been, our childhoods, the music in our lives. We confessed our fear and confusion. We became very good friends in a very short time. People at truck stops stared a bit at our unlikely quartet: the dapper Barney, the long-haired, slightly disheveled rocker, the young manager—and the old lady. We were a motley crew.

When we got to Denver, Warren was met by his bandmates, all of whom had creatively managed to arrive in time. Barney and I decided to stay over and go to their show before driving on. The crowd at the large club was a diverse group of men and women, mostly college age, but surprisingly welcoming to the older, rather lost-looking woman who joined them. I didn't give my full name, so I was on my own there yet was instantly included, invited by young strangers to join them as they found a good spot close to the stage. I later realized that some of their remarkable hospitality had been chemically induced, but at the time it didn't matter. I was in the midst of swaying, gyrating fans, not the jumping-bean Foo Fighters fans I was used to. It felt like what I imagined a Grateful Dead reunion would be.

The music we were all so grateful to hear was superb. Warren's bluesy, Joplin-like voice punctuated his virtuoso guitar playing. The audience screamed for encore after encore. The long night finally ended as the exhausted band left the stage. Barney and I said good-bye to our new friends and prepared for the last days of our journey. Along the way we stopped to listen to the rustling music the aspen trees made in the autumn breeze. We photographed scenic mesas and mountains as we passed through the Western states of this glorious country. Barney was happy to slow the pace after his marathon first few days and invited me to join him up front, where the wide windows yielded the best views. It was a very good lesson in geography and the perfect time to be reminded of the vastness and diversity of our country. It was a reminder to cherish it.

Several days after I arrived in Los Angeles, Warren's band played a show at the House of Blues. Lisa, David, and I met him before the show, and we laughed and reminisced about our unusual bus trip. Then we enjoyed a magnificent evening of music. At the end of the set list Warren called David to the stage for their last number, and they played a classic song that will never again have the impact it had that night. It was "Keep on Rockin' in the Free World."

Unforgettable.

WARREN HAYNES

Born: April 6, 1960, in Asheville, North Carolina

Gov't Mule (1994–present) and other bands (1982–present): Guitar, vocals

Genre: Southern Rock, hard rock, blues, blues-rock, jam

First Album: *Gov't Mule* (1995)

ELLEN TAYLOR

Mother of Warren Haynes
(Gov't Mule)

WHITE DOGWOOD BLOOMS DOTTED the winding, wooded roads just outside Asheville, North Carolina. Pink and fuchsia azaleas crawled over weathered gray fences, and tin mailboxes identified the owners of barns and vast fields where horses and cattle grazed. A catfish farm was announced by a crude wooden sign not far from the brook that rambled alongside the road. I opened the windows to feel the air, crisp and fresh, on the perfect spring morning.

I pulled into a driveway surrounded by clumps of daffodils in their waning bloom and walked to the modest house, where Ellen Taylor greeted me with a friendly welcome. Ellen, the mother of Warren Haynes, was eighty years old, lithe and straight, with shiny gray hair brushed away from her face and falling to her shoulders. She seemed genuinely happy to see me and to reflect on her past—"a full life, a great life."

I wanted to hear about the family that produced one of the finest musicians of our time. If you ask any guitar player to name the greatest aficionados of that instrument, you are certain to hear Warren Haynes's name at the top of the list. He has been playing in bands for over thirty years to great acclaim. The Allman Brothers added him to their lineup in the late '80s. He has made many guest appearances with the Dave Matthews Band and the Grateful Dead. And Gov't Mule, Warren's band, which was formed in the '90s, continues to sell out venues and to produce award-winning albums.

A 2015 episode of the PBS television show *Front and Center* featured Warren, his band, and a few guest artists playing before a small audience at the McKittrick Hotel in New York City. Watching it, I was mesmerized yet again by his complex, mysterious music. Is it symphonic? Celtic? Appalachian? Blues? Country? Perhaps it's all of those, masterfully combined to compel a person to listen closely. Now fifty-six, Warren has been playing for audiences large and small for forty-two years. Described by David Fricke of *Rolling Stone* as "possibly the hardest-working guitarist on the planet," he's released an album every year since 1995.

Was this where all that music started, I wondered, as Ellen took me inside. She brought tea and cookies to a cozy, wood-paneled room, where we sat comfortably and she told me her story.

Born in 1935 in a small town only thirty-five miles from her current home, Ellen was the fifth child of ten in a Polk County community where large families and low incomes were typical. "We grew up very poor, but we didn't know it," she says. Like the parents in all those other families, her father went to work and her mother stayed home with her large brood. When Ellen was only thirteen, her mother died, and the family was split up, the children sent to various relatives. It was a difficult time for Ellen, requiring adjustments she wasn't prepared for. But they managed. Seven of the ten siblings are still living, four of them in Polk County.

Ellen married her high school sweetheart, Edward Haynes, shortly after graduation, and they moved to New Orleans, where work was available in the oil fields. The young wife who had never traveled outside her county was greeted by an entirely new culture. A Baptist upbringing made her suspicious of Roman Catholics, and they were ev-

Warren & Ellen...

Springtime in Asheville

erywhere. Her culture shock was alleviated when she got an office job with the Yellow Pages company and made friends there. When she was only twenty, her first son, Tim, was born. Before five years had passed, she was the very young mother of three boys. Warren, the youngest, was born in 1960, and by then they had returned to Asheville.

Ellen raised Warren for the first seven years of his life. When she and Edward divorced, the boys went to live with their father and she remarried. She and her new husband, Bill Taylor, moved to nearby Greenville, where his own three children lived. "We did the best we could," she says. Now as she looks at her large family—her three children, her stepchildren, her grandchildren, and one great-grandchild—she is truly grateful for the solid relationships that have grown from some troubled times. But she doesn't give herself any credit. "I don't feel that I've always earned that. I haven't always been a good mother," she says.

We talked about the changing rules of parenthood. "I grew up in an era when children were to be seen and not heard," she recalls. "We were expected to do what we were told, without questioning anything." She believes that her strict expectations of her own children may have made life difficult for them. But she is full of praise for the parenting skills of her children now. "They all amaze me at what good parents they are," she says.

She doesn't sound like an inflexible parent when she describes Warren's early years. He was afflicted with multiple allergies—to grasses and pollens, wheat flour, and other foods. He was lactose intolerant. "He poured orange juice on his cereal," she laughs. Finding an appropriate diet was a constant challenge. It must have been even more difficult to find ways to entertain an energetic, athletic child inside the house while the other boys, unaffected by allergies, played in the open fields. Warren loved to be read to. He would construct his own stories and enlist Mama in playacting. He was the superhero and Ellen would be the unfortunate damsel in distress. Long before he started school he was reading on his own and could entertain himself.

Warren credits his mother for teaching him to read, for giving him a head start on learning and a love for words. His own poetry, lyrics, and ballads would not be too many years in the future.

He had a little red plastic guitar that he loved, and he strummed it along to the records he listened to. When his allergies made him ill and he found it hard to sleep, Ellen sat by him and played his favorite songs over and over on his record player.

We're seeing the birth of the artist here, aren't we? In the creative force Warren employed to concoct stories and dreams, and in his listening to music to relieve his anxiety and sickness. Of course, at the time, a busy mother wouldn't be thinking about that. She would be desperately hoping for him to be healthy and happy—and asleep.

Warren became an outstanding student, taking challenging classes and earning good grades. He was the family's academic star, destined for college. But, of course, music got in the way. Ellen recalls his learning to play a real guitar at around twelve. He was self-taught, with a little help from his older brothers. "I used to refer to them lovingly as the music police," Warren told me. They had collected thousands of vinyl albums and guided him to listen to the very best. "No, don't bother with that one," they would urge, "listen to this!" Soon he was forming his own band and at fourteen began sneaking into a little folk club in Asheville to hear as much music as he could. He heard folk music and appreciated the artists' storytelling. He heard Appalachian music and bluegrass and soaked up the locals' guitar-picking skills. He was inspired by their mastery of the magical strings on hollow wooden instruments. Soon word got out that the young boy who showed up so regularly and listened so intently could play guitar. "So they grabbed me up to play," Warren remembers, "and at that point everything changed. It was a tiny stage with room for only a few musicians, hardly even a drum kit or anything. But the power of live music in a small room was overwhelming. Playing in front of an audience was the most exciting thing ever." That was his "Aha!" moment.

His destiny was clear. Ellen recalls no one standing in his way with discouragement or advice to "be practical." She says his dad was always supportive and appreciated his talent. Years later she was in the audience when Edward joined Warren on the Ryman Auditorium stage in Nashville, and father and son sang a Hank Williams song. It was a proud moment for all of them.

Ellen has a big confession to make. She likes "easy music," the soothing kind that her granddaughter calls "dentist-chair music." "I grew up on country music, sad songs, heartbreaking songs, a soap opera kind of music." She's had enough of that. She doesn't enjoy loud rock music either. In fact, she's quite happy just listening to the calm background music of the Weather Channel, alternately amusing and appalling her grandchildren.

Warren suspects Ellen might be joking. "Music was always special in our family, never just background music." She was as encouraging as his father and brothers were, perhaps drawn to his talent as a story-teller. "I think she knew that I was intrigued by stories and thought if I didn't go into music I'd probably go into some sort of creative writing or journalism."

Perhaps by now, several months after our meeting, Ellen has turned off the weather music and has listened to *Ashes and Dust*, Warren's latest record. Because it features acoustic instruments, it has been called "folky," but the music is much more interesting than that. Is there such a thing as Appalachian jazz? Wailing fiddles, strong drum beats, and jazz guitar call the listener to remember days gone by—porch swings and times when "we were young and free." The music powerfully evokes the longing to return to a simpler time. If someone could invent an appropriate category for *Ashes and Dust*, it would surely win a Grammy.

The highlight of every year for all members of the Taylor and Haynes clans is the Christmas Jam. This twenty-seven year tradition, conceived and led by Warren, began in Asheville as a way to gather local musicians, bringing them all in from "the road" to return home for the holidays. Over the years it has expanded to a weekend festival and has become a significant fundraiser for Habitat for Humanity. Because of its impact, Warren has been honored with a key to the city and an official Warren Haynes Day. Ellen looks forward to it because she'll get to spend time with Warren's son, Hudson, the bright, affable little boy Warren and his wife, Stefani, adopted. They are raising him in a rural area about an hour outside New York City. But Christmas must always be spent in Asheville, for the Jam—and for Ellen.

Ellen worries, as all grandparents of our generation do, that Hudson will be spoiled. Although she is reassured by the fact that Warren's success has not been flaunted or mishandled, she knows that the fact that he waited so long for fatherhood might lead him to spoil his son. She says, "Hudson has anything he wants, and I don't think that's a good thing. I think you have to do without some things to appreciate what you've got. I pray about that a lot."

Grandmothers will worry, that much is guaranteed. And this is a very common double-edged sword. We are delighted and grateful that our sons' hard work has earned them the privilege of having what they want, but we like to tell ourselves that the years of deprivation we presented them with were better for them than their current prosperity. It may be a bit of humble hubris (Chapter 1 in my next book: "The Truth in Oxymorons").

Ellen's humility is genuine. Although she fed Warren's imagination by reading to him for hours to keep her housebound little boy happy, she didn't imagine that her child was a prodigy. She was young, uncertain, loving. But she will never claim to have influenced him at all. How different from young mothers of today! They seem to be frantic to fill the child's days with "enrichment opportunities," group activities, and early learning experiences, and to measure a child's every bit of progress as a sign of future success or an indication that outside help must be called in. Children are signed up for full calendars of "productive" activities, creating complicated schedules and frenzied arrangements for carpools. Perhaps Ellen and I were more fortunate to have felt comfortable with simple, uncomplicated lives. Our boys invented their entertainments and were free to explore types of music we found surprising. We may have given our best gifts passively. We didn't stand in the way.

Ellen thinks it is important for her children and grandchildren to have a sense of their family history. She has written "little booklets" for them about the times and places of her life. She wants them to hear about the grandmother they could never meet and a way of life that is lost.

She also writes the occasional poem. I found this one appropriate to our conversation:

A MOTHER'S PRAYER

A mother's prayer is never heard except
'tween her and God;
For all her children's needs and cares are
uppermost in her heart;
It matters not what path they took or
where their feet have trod.
She knows the ache from wanting their
happiness and safety from the start.

It matters not the choices made, whether
foolish or wise;
Let them cause no pain or harm to
others,
For each heartbreak they endure, she
cries.
To keep her offspring safe from harm is
the silent prayer of mothers.

The vagabond life of the touring musician may sound like a difficult, unstable choice to some. Yet musicians learn early that certain boundaries just aren't for them. They must go to new places to hear exotic sounds. They need to reach beyond their familiar surroundings to share what they have created with audiences who await them. They need to collaborate and meet with other music makers. Their office is a globe to be constantly explored.

It takes a special type of person to live that kind of life. The travel can be exhausting, the rules and customs of new places confusing, yet musicians seem to thrive on the rewards. Ellen, wise and thoughtful, wasn't terribly surprised that Warren chose New York City as his home for so many years. The boy from a small, bucolic town in North Carolina moved to the epicenter of art and culture, to a city rich in variety and experience, where every kind of music could be heard at its best. He loves the city's fast pace and palpable energy. Ellen loves hearing about the big city. She's curious about it but hasn't been there yet. Someday, perhaps.

Warren chose a wife, Stefani Scamardo, who seems to embody that New York verve. I assumed when I met her that she was a native New

At Ellen's home

Yorker, but in fact she grew up only a few miles from my Virginia home. She is instantly affable and exudes humor and a friendly, welcoming energy. She has been manager of Warren's bands and worked at Sirius XM Radio.

Warren has been touring, recording, writing, and producing for thirty-five years. He has defied the boundaries of musical categorization as he continues to experiment with new combinations of instruments and influences. The word "visionary" is often used to describe him. He has won a Grammy and was honored by the Recording Academy in 2012 with a Lifetime Achievement Award. His name is in the top tier of *Rolling Stone* magazine's One Hundred Greatest Guitarists of All Time. In addition, he received an honorary doctor of humane letters from UNC Asheville, which was bestowed in 2013 to show appreciation for his many years of work with Habitat for Humanity.

Fatherhood has enriched—and complicated—Warren's life over the past five years. "Everything changes," he sighs, "starting with what time you get out of bed, how tired you are." Beyond that he believes parenthood has also changed his creative process. "It changes the way you think about writing songs," he says. "I'm looking at things differently, through my eyes and his. It's like I have two perspectives on everything now." It might not be too long before Hudson joins him onstage. "He has great rhythm, great pitch," the proud papa brags. Hudson is already writing songs. Sometimes when Warren and Stefani ask what he's singing, he says, "Oh, I just made that up."

A musical icon, a devoted husband and father, and a beloved son. Yet to me Warren Haynes will always be the friend I found on a bus on 9/11. We shared our stories as we traveled from the horrific Ground Zero scenes to our safer havens: for him, a stage; for me, a family. We ate lunch at truck stops and talked some more as day rolled into evening. Finally, as midnight approached, I headed for my little bunk, pulled the curtains, and lay quietly as strange, sweet odors wafted from the back lounge. I slept really well.

Warren Haynes, the genius singer, composer, guitar maestro—the small-town country boy who conquered the world of music—will always be one of my favorites. And Warren and I would like to give Ellen Taylor some of the credit she has always refused.

VIGNETTE #9

PARTY ON, DAVE!

Entertainers are in the business of creating memories. On a stage, in front of a camera, or through their recordings they connect with an audience. Most of them confess that they find fulfillment in those shared moments when audience and artist celebrate sounds, images, and ideas together. Their goal is to ensure that we're all having a very good time.

   The entertainer I know best, my son, David, has extended this mission to his personal life. We call him "the host with the most." He loves to throw parties! A crab feast with delicacies flown in from the Chesapeake Bay, a pool party with German food, a lavish Halloween with acres of ghoulish props and eerie music are just some of the memorable events he's hosted. Many recall a New Year's Eve party at his studio that featured a '50s theme. Although I was one of the few in attendance who actually remembered those fashion-challenged years, I had enormous fun being surrounded again by saddle shoes, circle skirts, beehive hairdos, and Fonzie getups. I added rhinestone cat-eye glasses to my outfit as a nod to the past. The food, however, may have been less than authentic. Not a single Jell-O mold!

   David's love for costumed affairs goes way back to early childhood, when he declared Halloween his favorite holiday. At first my homemade

Which witch?

efforts were sufficient to satisfy his need for disguise. Later, though, he began urging me, months before October, to take him to a theatrical supply shop for a special one-of-a-kind mask or accessories. That was years before the mega-Halloween supply stores popped up in every suburban mall in the country.

In the '80s the Grohl Christmas party tradition began. The first year, Lisa, David, and I casually invited a few friends, most of whom were out of town for much of the year, to stop by on Christmas night. By then most of our friends had had enough family time to satisfy their obligations and were delighted to have an option for the evening. Also, nothing else was open! After our Christmas-afternoon feast we sliced the rest of the turkey, added some ham, filled bowls with chips, made a cheese platter, and welcomed our guests.

As the years went on and word spread, the guests and the party fare multiplied. Preparations began days before the event. Shrimp platters, hot crabmeat dip, layered taco spread, a whole ham, baskets of bread, and dozens of Christmas cookies filled our antique courtroom table, where Lisa's elaborate gingerbread houses served as the centerpiece. Hot buttered rum, coffee, sodas, and beer were served from the kitchen bar as Lisa's friends, David's family of local musicians, and my former students filled the house and spilled out onto the patio, where rented heaters sputtered uselessly against the cold December air.

In the Nirvana years, David's pal Jimmy, who knew how to affect a fearsome stance, manned the door, making sure the guests were bona fide friends. We invited our neighbors, hoping to prevent their concern about noise and ruling out police intervention. Those reunion nights are still recalled fondly—girls in sequins and velvet, guys in their best T-shirts, cameras flashing, music blasting.

I'm always surprised at how many backstage conversations lovingly recall those sadly discontinued Christmas fests. Recently a friend of David's reminded me of the year snow began to fall just as the door opened for the first guests. As it continued, it became apparent that our living room would become a dormitory for those who stayed long enough to be snowed in. There was plenty of ham for breakfast. A few who decided to head out spent the night sleeping on chairs in the waiting room of a nearby hospital, where they had safely and wisely parked their cars. They left unnoticed the next morning and traveled home on newly plowed roads.

Many years and many parties later, David invited friends and family to celebrate his fortieth birthday at Medieval Times. We ate large chunks of meat with our hands as stalwart knights, flags flying, galloped by in the arena below. It was silly, outrageous fun.

The ultimate party, the magnum opus of my "host with the most," was a London birthday celebration for me. My end-of-August birth date coincides with the last summer music festivals in the UK, so I have found myself there for many birthdays. One of them was unforgettable. In my London hotel I had just dressed for dinner when I was summoned to Jordyn and David's room for an early champagne toast. After popping the cork and pouring the bubbly, they took me to their balcony, which overlooked Hyde Park. "Look down there," David instructed. "There's a red double-decker bus. Do you see it?"

Parked in a shaded area just steps from our hotel stood the crimson carriage that awaited. It was my birthday bus! The three of us boarded and headed upstairs for the open-air seats. The other Foo Fighters and their wives joined us. Then came the members of the crew, who presented me with a birthday T-shirt portraying all their faces printed over an endearing message. When the band's management staff boarded, we had a full bus.

Our tour guide surprised us with facts and revelations about a city we thought we knew. There was much to learn about the rich history of the charming neighborhoods we drove through. As the daylight dimmed and we passed Kensington Palace and wound through Hyde Park, we sang Beatles songs and drank champagne. We watched the lights illuminate the theater district, where people in outdoor cafes looked up at us jealously and raised a glass. Ours was clearly the best party in town.

I don't remember the year, the age I was marking, or the menu of the birthday dinner that followed. But I vividly remember the absolute joy of seeing my favorite city unfold as my band family sang "Hey Jude" and celebrated my day. My fun-loving, thoughtful son knew that nothing could have made me happier. It was the best party of all.

AMY JADE WINEHOUSE

Born: September 14, 1983, in Southgate, London, England

Died: July 23, 2011

Amy Winehouse (2003–2011): Vocals, guitar, drums

Genre: Soul, pop

First Album: *Frank* (2003)

JANIS WINEHOUSE

Mother of
Amy Winehouse

"IT'S CALLED LIFE," **JANIS WINEHOUSE** said when early in our conversation she revealed that she has multiple sclerosis. And she said it many times thereafter: "I love life. Life is short. Enjoy it."

This despite the anguish and despair that accompanied the life of her superstar daughter, Amy, who died at age twenty-seven of alcohol poisoning. In her brief lifespan Amy Winehouse rose to international fame, winning awards and acclaim for her one-of-a-kind soulful voice and her daring songwriting. She was also notorious for her wild behavior, first with drugs and then with alcohol, her ongoing war with the paparazzi, and her determination to keep the world guessing about when she would show up and what state she would be in when she finally did. She tried the patience and exhausted the sympathies of fans, managers, and almost everyone else around her. Except for her father and her mother, Janis.

Janis Seaton was born in Brooklyn, New York, in 1955. Her father, Eddie, a man she adored, worked as a tailor. He took the family back to London, where he was from, before Janis was two years old. Her mother, Esther, seemed dissatisfied with everything about their lives and is described by Janis as a selfish, difficult woman. "To her, I was a bother," Janis said. "She would say, 'What are you doing? You know that's trouble. I can't handle it.' It was all about her."

The day before Janis married, Esther left Eddie for another man and was a no-show at Janis's wedding, putting a damper on what should have been a joyous occasion. Janis vowed then to be a good mother, to be everything her mother had not been. She would never put herself first.

Despite the lack of motherly attention and affection, Janis, her older brother, and her younger sister managed to stick together and have a somewhat normal childhood. She admits that she was a less than stellar student and often looked for mischief with her friends. She firmly asserted her independence at seventeen, when she set out for Miami, Florida, on her own. Having just finished training as a pharmacy technician, she found a job at a hospital and enjoyed the tropical weather and her new life as an independent working girl. After she returned to London she would begin planning the next phase of her education.

But first she met Mitch Winehouse, a gregarious, fun-loving guy who loved to sing, loved to entertain. When Janis married Mitch she became part of a loud, exuberant family. Weekly family dinners featured games and music—always music, especially jazz. Mitch's mother, Cynthia, became the mother Janis had never had, caring and fun-loving. Later, Cynthia was Amy's number-one fan and the only person in the family Amy would occasionally listen to.

Amy was born in 1983, three years after her brother, Alex, so by then Janis had learned the basics of mothering. But she soon found that none of those applied to the force that was Amy. From a young age Amy challenged authority, railed against structure, and was in constant motion, earning the nickname "Hurricane Amy." Janis recalled Amy's tempestuous early days and later rebellions in her book, *Loving Amy* (2014). She writes, "My life was spent constantly developing new strategies to get her to do the simplest things, from brushing her teeth before going to bed to getting her uniform on for school in the morning."

It was exhausting, and Janis faced the challenges on her own much of the time because Mitch often worked late, starting and building several businesses. The determined mother tried reasoning with her daughter, but Amy would escape, refusing to sit still long enough for an explanation of what was expected of her. At Friday night family dinners, however, the squirmy little rebel would transform into Grandma's helper, serving her parents then clearing the table, eager to please and be of help to her beloved Cynthia.

In school settings she couldn't concentrate or sit still. She would burst out singing in a loud voice when she was bored. She considered "don't do it" a dare and became reckless and unmanageable. Janis and Mitch spent hours in principals' offices looking for guidance but were usually told to find another school.

Janis and Mitch knew that Amy was clearly intelligent and very creative. The poetry that Janis saved over the years shows a child adept with language and able to grasp mature concepts. Amy carried a notebook with her everywhere and wrote prolifically: songs, poems, and lists. She loved to order things in lists even as she refused order in her life. And she was always singing—at family events, out her bedroom window, everywhere. When Amy was six her parents enrolled her in a once-a-week program called Stagecoach. At the first recital program the tiny diva amazed her parents and everyone else there with her incredible voice. Janis knew then that her ill-behaved, uncooperative daughter responded to music even as she refused all other types of instruction.

Her school reports complained of a lack of focus and an inability to sit still and to concentrate. She failed to cooperate or to comply with rules and expectations. But she had that voice, that amazing voice. She lasted longest at the special-arts schools that featured training in acting and music. When she was eleven she performed in *Grease* as Rizzo (who else?!) but was furious that she hadn't been cast as Sandy.

When she was older she looked back on one particular school with favor, the Sylvia Young Theatre School, where serious artists-to-be went for their early training. Her unique, soulful voice so impressed Sylvia Young that Young gave her many opportunities to sing and per-

Young Amy

Before the fame

form, as related by Mitch Winehouse in his book, *Amy, My Daughter* (2012). Amy appeared in a sketch on BBC2's comedy program *The Fast Show*. She was paid to stand on a ladder for half an hour in a production of *Don Quixote,* and she had a ten-minute monologue in a play at Hampstead Theatre.

But even at the Sylvia Young school she refused to follow the few simple rules that could have kept her there. She chose the forbidden chewing gum and hoop earrings, things it would seem easy to forgo, over the experience and training she was offered. She dared the system to accept her as she was.

Meanwhile, Amy's family life had its own challenges. When Janis learned that her husband's late hours and weekends away from home were not always for business but for another woman, she was distraught. Janis and Mitch's impending divorce, however, did not sever the strong bond she and the children shared with Cynthia, Mitch's mother, who continued to help support Janis during the difficult time ahead. A newly single mom with two needy children, Janis was midway through the courses for her college degree. Her days were long and challenging—attending classes, caring for her children, preparing food ahead of time for the nights when she had late sessions, making sure all of Alex's and Amy's needs were met. When the kids' lights finally went out at night, she opened her books to study. Janis was awarded a bachelor's of pharmacy degree when Amy was twelve. She began a year of training that required traveling to towns outside London. Her work hours were extended, her responsibilities doubled. She hoped that the example she was setting for Amy of hard work and achievement would be noticed, but it seemed to have little effect.

Amy's "adolescent" rebellion had begun in primary school, so her harried teachers and weary parents stood by as she sabotaged more of their efforts to make her life easier. When Janis confronted her fifteen-year-old daughter about drinking, Amy replied, "Don't worry, Mommy. I'm sorry, Mommy. I'm OK." That would continue to be her response to her mother's fears over the years.

In 2000 a significant breakthrough occurred when Amy was asked to sing with the National Youth Jazz Orchestra. She was sensational. The petite young girl with her powerful, sultry voice surprised all who heard her. There was a maturity, a soulful intensity to her interpretations of classic standards. She sang "The Nearness of You," one of her father's favorites, better, he said, than Ella or Sarah or Billie Holiday. She was that good—even at sixteen.

Her work with the jazz orchestra and occasional performances in pubs attracted attention, and in 2001, when Amy was seventeen, record companies began sending advance men to offer her deals. Janis was worried. She knew that the naughty little girl who had defied her parents' expectations and her school's rules hadn't changed her attitude to authority. Her little Amy was still Amy, reckless, headstrong, and unpredictable. People in the music industry wanted her voice. Janis wondered what else they would get.

Amy's response to her early success was just as Janis feared. After signing a four-year deal and receiving a generous advance, she balked at meetings and anything else that resembled structure or authority. She promised to go into a studio to work on new music but wouldn't show up on time. Or wouldn't show up at all. The recording equipment was moved to her house, but even that made little difference.

Because of Amy's age, Janis and Mitch needed to be involved in the business of signing contracts and receiving money. Mitch reentered Amy's life full-time. Janis had no objection. She was ill with what would soon be diagnosed as multiple sclerosis. As her symptoms multiplied and her energy diminished, she awaited a final diagnosis and establishment of a treatment regimen. It was terrible timing. Still, she did all she could to stay involved with Amy and help her find her way along this very challenging new path. One highlight of that period for Janis was attending a show at the Cobden Club, where Amy sang jazz standards. Annie Lennox had come to hear Amy and was impressed. So was Janis. A year later Janis would see her little girl's image enlarged to billboard size as she drove to work. Now that was a moment!

At eighteen Amy moved out of the family house into her own apartment. She had always been independent, and eighteen is certainly an accepted age for leaving the nest. But Janis feared that independence combined with round-the-clock freedom could be trouble for Amy. She tried to be subtle in her monitoring of her daughter but became concerned when it was clear that Amy was smoking a lot of pot and being more careless about appointments. Besides, the apartment looked like a war zone. It was always a terrible mess.

In the garden with Janis

Showing me her keepsakes

Amy's self-destructive behaviors multiplied. She drank to excess, often before going onstage, which Janis saw as a sign that she had no confidence in her talent. Her performances ranged from brilliant to disastrous, and she was a PR nightmare, insulting journalists and inviting even more criticism. She pulled away from Janis, unavailable for visits or phone calls, closing herself off from those who loved her, always just out of reach. Janis describes this heartbreaking period in *Loving Amy*. It's painful to read about a mother who had to stand by as her beautiful, talented child became hopelessly addicted and terrifyingly out of control.

"Rehab," the song that propelled Amy to the tops of charts everywhere, revealed the hopeless state of affairs the family faced. Amy would not be told what to do. She would say, "No."

Repeatedly.

In the last years of Amy's life, even Cynthia, the strict, no-nonsense grandmother, was helpless. When she confronted Amy, the response she got was "I don't have a problem." Even after admitting to Janis that she had tried cocaine and heroin, Amy shrugged off all concern. "I'm fine, Mummy. Don't worry about me." When Mitch took her to a clinic to detox and dry out, she signed herself out after fifteen minutes. She would do that many times.

Drugs, alcohol, canceled shows, embarrassing performances. It would seem that nothing more could be added to the turbulent mix. But there were two more factors to come, bulimia and Blake Fielder-Civil, who became Amy's husband.

Amy's attraction to Blake was immediate and powerful. Their three-year relationship was filled with drama, some of it violent, earning them the nickname "the modern-day Sid and Nancy." They celebrated their happiness with dangerous drugs and moved from apartments to hotels and back to escape detection. They pushed friends and family away. Janis, worried about Amy's weight loss and her dependence on a man Janis knew nothing about, was afraid. Her anxiety began to affect her health. Mitch continued to try to intercede, having Amy admitted to more clinics and hospitals, but to no avail. They worried that Amy would die.

The dizzying ups and downs of those years are hard to fathom, especially now, as Janis is able to smile at the good memories. Of Amy rushing into her arms for long, childlike hugs. Of Amy on her doorstep the morning after winning the Ivor Novello award. "Here it is, Mum. It's for you!" When Amy received several Grammys in 2008, she called Mitch and Janis to the stage for hugs. "I love you, Mum," she said. When she received a Brit Award, she said, "I'm just glad my mum and dad are here." She never withheld her affection for her parents. But she wouldn't listen to them, heed their warnings, accept their advice, or acknowledge their concern.

During the Blake years Janis had to stop reading newspapers and magazines. Seeing photos of her skeletal, disheveled daughter and reading reports of scandalous, drug-fueled behavior was too hard. She was a powerless bystander. Mitch continued to schedule Amy's admission to rehab facilities, but Blake and Amy always managed to have drugs smuggled in. Exasperating!

When Blake was sent to prison for an assault that didn't involve Amy, she was a bit more reachable, and after a series of disastrous performances she agreed to try Subutex to help her come off drugs. She spent some time in the Caribbean and gained a little weight. Janis was encouraged by her progress. She flew to Saint Lucia to see Amy perform at a jazz festival. But though now free of drugs, Amy was drinking all the time. She was drunk onstage, and the audience booed. It was humiliating. When Janis tried to broach the subject, Amy cut her off. "Don't, Mom. I'm too embarrassed."

In 2009 Amy divorced Blake and was no longer using drugs, but she was in a constant state of inebriation. Tours and shows had to be canceled due to her extreme alcoholism. There was another short rehab stay, then live-in bodyguards were hired when she insisted on going home. "Don't bug me," she'd say. "I'll sort it when I want. I did it with drugs. I can do it." But this last addiction was too powerful and struck the final blow. Amy died of alcohol poisoning at age twenty-seven.

Janis had been with Amy the night before she died. She had told Amy she loved her. In the painful days that followed, Janis endured a mother's worst fate, grieving the loss of a child. Family and friends gathered to comfort her. They were constantly surrounded by a parade of photographers and reporters. Somehow days led to weeks, weeks to months. Janis got through.

Three years later, when I met her, Janis was choosing to "love life." Twenty years of extreme highs and lows taught her to value every positive moment she can claim. Her son, Alex, had just become a parent, and she looked forward to helping the new grandson, her first, thrive. She was realistic about the limitations of her MS, but insisted on traveling for an upcoming Caribbean cruise and a reunion with friends in Florida. She walked with a cane, but her new husband, Richard Collins, was quick to provide an arm to support her and a great amount of humor to keep her optimistic.

In 2011 Janis and Mitch created the Amy Winehouse Foundation, a multipronged charity. The foundation promotes drug education programs in schools. It is their hope that at-risk children can be discovered early and helped. The charity also offers studio time and professional support to young musicians who show talent, and provides scholarship grants to "deserving students from disadvantaged families for educational opportunities."

To raise money and awareness for the charity, in 2014 Janis put down her cane, strapped on a parachute, and jumped out of a plane. She is determined to translate her grief into actions to help others. Her studies and life experiences have helped her understand the destructive nature of addiction; her bravery and optimism drive her to assure that her efforts will make a positive difference. Both Janis and Mitch have pledged the profits from their books to the foundation, and they regularly travel to visit the centers and programs they have established.

As I left Janis's sunny London garden, I marveled at the strength of her optimism that rose above the residual sadness, at the spirit of this woman who still insists on loving life, who still says, "It's called life—and it's short. Live it!"

VIGNETTE #10

PRIDE AND JOY

"You must be so proud!"

Rock moms hear that often, from friends and strangers alike. Usually the comment follows a Grammy win, a White House performance, or a television special. All are certain to produce the undeniable, almost instinctual response: a mother's pride in her child's achievement.

It should be noted, though, that most of us secretly value unreported acts of generosity and kindness even more than prestigious trophies. We are most proud of commitments to family or community that reveal the real essence of the man or woman our child has become, that show us "It's times like these you learn to live again . . . /It's times like these you learn to love again," as the songwriter I'm so proud of put it.

The goofy, sweet, forgetful, charismatic child who became a famous "Fighter of Foo," as David Letterman loved to say, continues to surprise me with his essential goodness. I'll show a few examples of proud moments to serve as examples of why mothers cry when they are happy.

Ten years ago, in a little-known area of Tasmania, a gold mine collapsed, trapping a small crew of miners for two weeks. When it was determined that a hatch could be drilled through the rock to deliver life-supporting food and water, the miners were given a bit of hope. But they had a further request. They asked for Foo Fighters music. Their wish was granted: the music was delivered, along with a note of encouragement from David—and a promise of tickets and beers at any Foo Fighters show in the world, giving them something to celebrate, something to look forward to. The deal was sealed several months later, at a show in Sydney, Australia. They were further treated to a song in their honor, "The Ballad of the Beaconsfield Miners," which appeared on the next album. This story has been reported a few times. It is, however, most significant to me. It demonstrates that the child I hoped would have compassion learned his lessons well.

A family situation will serve as another example. At the school attended by David's two oldest girls, the annual Daddy-Daughter Dance is a not-to-be-missed yearly highlight. Although Superdad gets up at 5:30 a.m. to make breakfast, pack lunches, check backpacks, and drive his girls to school every day when he's not on tour, there is no acceptable excuse for failing to put on a jacket and escort two little girls in their new party dresses to this event—even when a band tour puts him on the other side of the world on the night the dance is scheduled.

Here's how a Superdad handled it: David played a show in Australia, ran to the airport, boarded a plane for a fifteen-hour flight to LA, took Violet and Harper to the gala, danced the night away with one on each arm, drove them home, kissed them good night, and immediately boarded another flight back to Australia. He arrived just in time to run onstage for his next show.

Exhausting? It's hard to imagine the jet-lag effects of a marathon like that. Furthermore, since that night he hasn't mentioned this way-above-the-call-of-duty act of fatherly dedication. It's just what he does. That's the kind of thing I'm so proud of, even in awe of. That's my very good son.

My most recent proud moment occurred when David was honored as a Champion for Children at a benefit for the Los Angeles Child and Family Guidance Center. It was the culmination of an important project that was instituted when a member of the organization's staff asked David for some ideas about using music to help at-risk teens. His ideas became a

commitment. He spent the next several months working with young people who were dealing with serious issues. His first meeting with them was described by Dr. Brette Genzel-Derman, a program director at the institute, in the speech she gave to honor him: "When he walked into the group room, he basically took over the joint. He looked each teen in the eye and shook their hands. He wasn't distracted or rushed. He was *present*. And frankly, when you're dealing with teens that are facing depression, anxiety, low self-esteem, and suicidal ideation, well, it's damn important to be present. He treated those kids with so much respect and kindness—it took my breath away."

Dr. Genzel-Derman described how David had given the teens a voice to translate their feelings and ideas to lyrics, which they set to music as he empowered them to create. They named themselves Sonic Teens, and on that special night at the Skirball Center they rushed to the stage with their new mentor to share with an audience of several hundred adults in black tie what they had accomplished. They lined up across the stage, two girls and two boys, and began to play and sing, confidence rising with each phrase. The shy, green-haired girl sitting on a chair, microphone in hand, slowly raised her eyes to the audience. She smiled tentatively as her voice went from a whisper to full volume. The young guitarist next to her transformed as he looked from her to David to the audience. Soon it was clear he was having the time of his life. A young boy and girl stood, stiffly at first, also singing. Then the boy stepped forward with rap lyrics as the music continued behind him. They moved and swayed with the music, and their smiles broadened as they realized how completely engaged their audience had become. Throughout the performance David sat with them, playing his guitar, not conducting or directing, just being a part of their ensemble, a part of their song.

Not long before this memorable evening, as their weekly songwriting sessions were coming to an end, the newly empowered Sonic Teens came up with a plan of their own. They arranged a secret studio session and recorded their own personal lyrics to "My Hero," which they played for David as a song of thanks at their last session. They watched their hero's proud, emotional response and were assured that they had made an impact on him as he had on them. They had learned to speak through their music, joyously, confidently, and profoundly.

Now look who's proud! Everyone!

JOSH WINSLOW GROBAN

Born: February 27, 1981, in Los Angeles, California

Josh Groban (1997–present): Vocals, piano, drums, percussion

Genre: Classical, musical theater, original songs

First Album: *Josh Groban* (2001)

LINDY GROBAN

Mother of
Josh Groban

LINDY GROBAN HAS PROBABLY NEVER referred to her son Josh as a
rock star. He's been difficult to label since he began recording fifteen
years ago. Seven albums (and thirty million copies) later, he was nominated for a 2016 Grammy for Best Traditional Pop Vocal Album. (Tony
Bennett and Bill Charlap won the award.) His body of work continues
to defy classification, as does his voice. He may be a tenor. Or a baritone.
One thing is certain: he has a growing audience of loyal fans. And they
don't care about categories. They just want more music.

At a 2016 concert at the Dolby Theatre in Los Angeles, in which
he featured the songs from his most recent album, *Stages,* I chatted
with the excited folks who were lined up for the sold-out show. They
bragged about the number of his shows they had attended and how far
they had traveled to see him. Like Grateful Dead fans in the '80s who
followed that band from city to city, Grobanites exude a palpable enthusiasm (even if they are less colorfully attired). Lindy Groban and her
husband, Jack, were in that Dolby audience, too, often acknowledged
by the charming, affable entertainer they had so lovingly raised.

Lindy always knew that music was fun. Her mother sang to her and
showed her photos from her early, short-lived vaudeville career. She
was the little auburn-haired girl who would jump out of the chorus line
and tip her top hat, revealing a mop of curls. Lindy did not follow suit;
she had no early stage career, no top hat. She grew up in LA, the only

The music begins

child of the ebullient mother she adored and a hardworking, enterprising father she loved and respected. Born in 1943, Lindy's postwar childhood was "wonderfully simple—riding bikes, roller skating, running carefree and barefoot all summer."

In those days the LA public schools assured that all students had access to the best in the arts. A ballet, an opera, and a Philharmonic concert were provided to middle school students each year. Lindy can still picture scenes from *Madame Butterfly* and has fond memories of the classical ballet *Coppelia*. Her early exposure to the arts is something she has not forgotten, and she and Josh are working to reestablish some of the valuable programs, all of which were discontinued decades ago in the name of budget priorities.

Those field trips had ended by the time Josh was a student in the LA school system. He was fortunate, though, to have dedicated parents who more than compensated for the loss. As he introduces his songs onstage, he tells stories of family outings to art galleries and symphonies. The child who began playing and composing music well before he was school age was captivated by the varieties of sights and sounds he encountered on those excursions.

"He was not an easy baby," Lindy recalls. "He didn't take naps for more than a heartbeat," and his supercharged energy was a shock to his mother, who was thirty-seven when he was born. (Hers was offensively labeled a geriatric pregnancy.) Her task was to channel his high energy, to engage the "busy brain" of her talented child. When the toddler, still in diapers, climbed up to sit on the bench of their Casio keyboard, flipped on the bossa nova beat, and began to discover chords and rhythms, she knew theirs would be a musical journey. Josh recalls putting on shows and making funny movies with his brother. He appreciates the creative freedom he was given and the enthusiastic audience provided by his trumpet-player dad and art-teacher mom. His artistic urges were assisted by his ability to read early and his advanced vocabulary. This child was really bright! Surely he would be a success in school!

But that was not the case. The sweet, funny boy who never acted out and was never rebellious or discourteous was not a "good student." Despite his excellent memory, he would look out the window (something teachers love to point out as a major sin) and not finish a test. He had a hard time organizing tasks and materials but loved studying Japanese. He was an excellent writer—with deplorable handwriting. Those of us who recognize these patterns can predict the school's response: "He's not applying himself. He's too easily distracted. He just needs to focus." Yet the same lollygagger will come home and spend hours with a guitar or piano or drums, intently focused, creatively engaged, no longer distractedly looking out the window. That part of the pattern is never seen by the teachers.

Josh's school years were trying times for Lindy. She was too often soothing his wounds after his failures, making sure to also note each moment of success. His "Aha!" moment came in the seventh grade. Josh had convinced a teacher to start a lunchtime drama group and create a cabaret show. Lindy drove him to rehearsal and was instructed by her son to remain in the car with a book. It was a rare rainy day, but through the closed windows and the rain, Lindy heard a voice that compelled her to go to the auditorium door. "I think that's Josh," she said to herself. "My Lord, I think that's Josh!" Hearing him croon "'S Wonderful" was a genuine surprise. Before that moment she had never heard Josh sing alone. He had joined his Cub Scout group in some singalongs, but he'd never sung around the house. She had no indication that he would one day be a Grammy-nominated vocalist or perform to a sold-out crowd in front of an orchestra at the Dolby. Like many of the musically talented children portrayed in this book, Josh found his instrument around age twelve. His instrument was his voice.

As Josh's young soprano voice matured and deepened, another Cub Scout parent, Seth Riggs, took notice and became his vocal coach. Seth, who had worked with Michael Jackson and Jennifer Lopez, could recognize talent.

Josh surprised Lindy again by pleading with her to let him take adult improv classes at a comedy venue. The classes would require long drives at a late hour. "Please, Mom, just let me try!" He had always made people laugh. Even as a young child he had a sophisticated wit. So she relented. Those of us who have heard Josh's hilarious vocal tweets on Jimmy Kimmel's show or enjoyed his many comedic performances on TV say, "Thanks, Lindy!"

Soon Josh was enrolled in LACHSA (Los Angeles County High School for the Arts). The years of searching for an appropriate school ended. Lindy has some advice for parents who know that their children "learn differently": "If you have a creative child, you must advocate for your child. The school must create self-confidence, a sense of value. It must assure the child that he or she is capable. It must be engaging, exciting. It must not marginalize or stigmatize."

During his high school years Josh attended Interlochen Arts Camp, in Michigan, where he thrived. He loved the "pure magic" of the place and now goes back to speak with the campers and entertain them. Josh told me that Interlochen and LACHSA shaped him as an artist and as a man, because he "met friends like me and felt most myself for the first time in my life."

After high school Josh enrolled at Carnegie Mellon University, but his education was cut short when his vocal coach recommended him as a stand-in at a rehearsal for an ailing Andrea Bocelli. That led to an invitation to sing at the 1999 inaugural of Gray Davis as California governor. And *that* eventually led to a full-time career marked by success after success.

Could Lindy and Jack step back and relax once Josh skipped university to focus on his singing career? Of course not. As a minor, he was still emotionally and legally their child. She describes the music business as "a difficult world. We had to learn [it], and we went through the looking glass to an alternate universe. We had to be quick studies. We had to protect him—he was seventeen—but we didn't know how." They soon realized that many others wanted influence and control over Josh, and nobody wanted the parents around, something Lindy could truly understand. So it was a delicate dance. In 2001 the dance ended when his debut album, *Josh Groban,* was released. It went double platinum. Two years later his second album, *Closer,* hit number one on the *Billboard* charts. In 2005 Josh received his first Grammy nomination for Best Male Pop Vocal Performance.

When she was in college, Lindy had made a life-changing, low-budget trip to Europe with a friend, and now she saw Josh traveling the world at the same age she'd been. She had been a "museum junkie," enchanted by Paris, Berlin, and Salzburg, not minding cheap hotels and overnight trains that would provide a night's rest. It was her time of freedom, a breathtaking adventure into worlds of art and culture. She hoped Josh would love it as she had.

In the fifteen years since his first album, Josh has recorded six more. He continues to tour, compose, and collaborate, and to act on TV and in film. In November 2016, Josh achieved a lifetime dream starring as Pierre in the new Broadway musical *Natasha, Pierre, and the Great*

At home with Lindy

Backstage at the Dolby Theatre

Comet of 1812, where both he and the production opened to excellent reviews. He and his family continue to oversee the foundation they created ten years ago, Find Your Light. Its formation was inspired by Josh's testimony before a congressional subcommittee in support of the National Endowment for the Arts, after which he decided to focus his charitable work on arts education. His foundation has raised millions of dollars, which has been directed to arts programs in underserved communities. Josh often talks about Find Your Light at his shows and invites the children who've participated in its programs to stand up and be acknowledged. "That is one of the gifts his success has given me as a mom," says the proud and grateful Lindy. Despite his more than full-time professional schedule, he visits the schools where his funds are in action, encouraging, inspiring, and joining the young artists in their endeavors. He really means to make a difference.

When there is time, all the Grobans relax together at their peaceful island retreat. Chris Groban, the younger of Lindy's "two extraordinary children," joins them. He excelled in the film-production program at USC and now directs commercials and music videos as well as assisting with film projects for Find Your Light. They play board games, go hiking or kayaking, and play with their dogs. Simple things, Lindy says.

Family has been important throughout their journey and continues to be so. "We're a strong family," Lindy says. She loves knowing that the bonds have grown stronger through the years. Lindy understands and appreciates her place in the lives of her artistic sons. "They need to know that you're always there, a safe place to go. You may not have all the answers, but you're there to listen. And if you're asked for advice, you'll give it."

And Josh, who describes his mother as "an anchor for my brother and me and the strongest person I know," still listens, too.

'S wonderful, isn't it?

VIGNETTE #11

MOTHER'S DAY

It's Mother's Day weekend and I'm thinking about all the mothers I've met in the past year, hoping their musical sons and daughters have a day off, or an hour off, to be with them and honor their special contributions. We moms of musicians have had to do it differently. Yes, we did carpools and soccer games and PTA bake sales, but many of us faced contentious battles at some point as school began to encroach on the time our kids insisted belonged to THE MUSIC. How did we affect their choices at those tense times? Or did we just not matter?

I believe we all saw it coming very early on. It was clear our kids were wired a little bit differently. On one hand they seemed typical, running for the school bus with their half-finished homework assignments stuffed into their backpacks with their gym shorts and lunch bags. On the other hand, their obsessive interest in listening to, talking about, composing, and playing music became at some point more important than school. They got less sleep, earned worse grades, made friends outside their neighborhood circles. They looked less and less like the Norman Rockwell poster children we had planned on.

As mothers, we often felt alone. We didn't know what to do, and we flew solo most of the time, without flight manuals or guidebooks. Many of us struggled through these challenges pre-Internet. Quite a few of us were single parents. Many of us had little or no money.

What we had were kids who were really good, really early on, at the music they were obsessed with. It was take it or leave it (meaning they would leave)—and most of us took it, not knowing what "it" was, and tried to hang on.

I honestly think you country-and-western music parents had it easy. Your kids wanted a big hat, some boots, maybe a little fringe, and a guitar. Those of us with punk rock progeny faced more daunting options. Mohawks! Tattoos! Shredded jeans with more holes than fabric. Not exactly wholesome photo ops for sending to Grandma. And unlike country music, the sounds emanating from our rockers' practice rooms were jarringly new and a bit terrifying. They pounded their drums mercilessly, screaming angry lyrics to fast-paced songs that were a far cry from the Rodgers and Hart ditties of our youth. This was new territory.

Our children had latched on to other fads, such as skateboards or video games, with their friends. But those were passing fancies, never penetrating deeply like their music. This music thing was undeniable, permanent, whether we chose to acknowledge it or not.

Somewhere down the line, the word "focus" became a mantra for teachers and parents. It was the key to success in lessons, in making good grades, in finding a better life. Our children were bombarded by this advice. And focus they did. Just not on *Silas Marner* or algebra. Our dilemma was different from that of other parents of struggling students. Do we admire the attribute or try to change the game? And does it matter?

Most of us did what we could to help them. Some of us just stayed out of the way. And almost all of us are enjoying this Mother's Day with grateful, loving, financially secure children and the grandchildren they've added to this happy mix.

What about the others? What happened to the practical, sensible women who hired therapists and tutors and paid private-school tuition and listened to the world of advice they were given by husbands, family members, and friends? What happened to their prodigy? I guess we'll never know. There are probably a few lawyers out there who show up at arena rock shows and would trade their BMWs for an hour onstage with a guitar. There are producers and agents and publicists who wear a tie to please Dad yet still would rather have gone on tour with a band. There are probably a few cases where there was so much hurt, so much damage done that the family relationship was severed. I suspect that was the reason some musicians turned me away instantly when I invited them to be part of my project. And I know one mother who, despite our friendly relationship, just couldn't bear to go public with the drama and pain of those years of her life.

To all of us I say, a "Happy Mother's Day!" Now why doesn't one of our geniuses write a Mother's Day song and line up all our sons and daughters "We Are the World"–style to serenade us?

ADAM LEVIN

Born: October 8, 1987, in Los Angeles, California

X Ambassadors (2009–present): Drums, percussion

Genres: Alternative rock, indie rock

First Studio Album: *VHS* (2015)

JUDY KAHN

Mother of Adam Levin
(X Ambassadors)

JUDITH SANDWEISS GREW UP just outside Detroit, Michigan, in a two-piano house. Her father, who had spent a term at Juilliard before going to law school, was a serious musician. Her older sister began playing with the Detroit Symphony Orchestra when she was twelve. Each day began with one of them practicing on the living room piano as the other played in the basement. Judy, still tucked in bed, believed that waking up to Chopin exercises meant oatmeal for breakfast; Bach indicated that eggs would be on the menu. It was her morning game.

Her own piano lessons yielded no treats. "I hated it. I wasn't good at it, and I couldn't sit still. I was a mover." So at five she began studying ballet.

"No tap dancing?" I asked.

Judy's response indicated a harsh reality of the dance world. "When I was a kid, if you were a talented dancer you did ballet. If you couldn't succeed in that you moved down to tap or jazz, both considered lesser arts."

Her attraction to ballet is hard to explain. "Ballet is no fun," she says. "It's very serious and very, very hard." Yet, a few years later she would choose dance training over family vacations, continuing to "not have fun." Why? "I was good at it. I loved it, and it ended up being all I ever really wanted to do." Making a commitment to dance requires "ten years of hard training, and if you're not in a ballet company by the time you're twenty, it will be really hard after that." The working life span of a dancer is short, similar to that of a football player or other elite athlete, she tells me.

Judy defied all the odds and worked in ballet, performing and teaching, into her late forties. At twelve she joined the Detroit City Ballet. After graduating early from high school, she went to New York to dance with the Harkness Ballet. Later she was with the Oakland Ballet and the Los Angeles Dance Theater. When she wasn't performing, she was teaching dance at colleges and universities. These days, sidelined by hip replacements (and replacements of those replacements), this incredibly young-looking sixty-year-old mom is in the audience rather than on the stage. And now it's as the mother of an emerging rock star, Adam Levin, the drummer for X Ambassadors.

Adam is the youngest of the three sons from Judy's twenty-year marriage to Alan Levin. Aaron, the oldest, played drums and guitar as a kid and was a serious, self-reliant scholar who "raised himself," according to his mother. "Homework, always done; deadlines, always met ahead of time." For his university education he chose Berkeley, where his father had earned a PhD while his mother danced with the Oakland Ballet, and he has remained in the Bay Area, working for the San Francisco Symphony as their webmaster. He still finds time to play drums with several bands, and he and his wife recently had a daughter, whom Judy looks forward to taking to ballets someday.

Danny, the second son, also loved music. He played guitar and drums, but it took a longer time to find a field that held his interest. Now the father of Miles, Judy's first grandson, he thinks he's struck gold—literally! He has a business that involves taking people to dig areas and teaching them how to mine.

All three boys went to Los Angeles schools, taking advantage of the magnet programs. Adam attended schools with strong music programs and played guitar with Walter Reed Middle School's enviable jazz band. In his humble assessment he was a much better drummer than guitarist, but he was one of the few who could read music, a requirement for the jazz band. Adam says his early musical training—beginning with violin lessons, moving to guitar and drums, and even including a short oboe interval—were not all happy moments. He only felt relaxed and

The early years

A benchmark moment!

happy with drumsticks in hand. Yet he didn't seem destined to be a hardcore, head-banging rock star. He was a sweet boy, thoughtful, humble, low-key. Judy recalls three-year-old Adam at the dinner table with his parents and his much older brothers. Adam would turn to one of them and say, "So, how was your day?"

In retrospect, Judy sees that the thoughtful child became an excellent team player, an admirable attribute for a band member. "He doesn't want to be a star; he's not looking for attention," she notes. She observes that this personality trait made him a good fit for his current band, X Ambassadors. Sam Harris, the talented, affable singer, takes the lead gracefully, onstage and in interviews, which seems just fine with Adam. Brother Danny concludes, "I don't think Adam wants to be a rock star; he just loves being a musician."

I first met Adam at a holiday party when he was in high school. Adam was excited to talk to David, but he also really wanted to talk to me to get the inside story on the "drummer who made it." I didn't realize at the time that he was charting his own course. His insightful questions simply indicated to me that he was a curious, very smart boy who was being most polite by engaging in a lengthy conversation with the oldest person in the room. I thought he was adorable. A short time after that party David gave Adam his old drum set when he was switching to a new kit. The starstuck teen drummer was excited and grateful for the generosity of one of his idols and began to play with renewed intensity.

Soon I was hearing his drums almost daily on the other side of my garden wall as he and my next-door neighbor and a few others announced to the world that the next Led Zeppelin was about to land—loudly! I also heard his exasperated mother's tales of the previously cooperative, compliant child who had suddenly drawn the line. He refused to show up for a yoga class to fulfill his high school PE requirement. Because he failed yoga he had to take ping-pong at a local college to get his high school diploma before he could move on to the New School in New York for university. Something about the bravely quiet rebellion of failing yoga made me like Adam even more, and I have followed his career ever since. In addition, the fact that ping-pong and yoga played a crucial role in the path of a child's education stands high on my list of Top Ten Absurdities in American Education.

Those high school years were often challenging for the mother and son. Adam told me about the struggles that ensued as he reached his difficult early teens, which is about the age when most of the musicians I've talked to made their commitment to playing forever. Adam says that's a "sensitive period, when you start to have your own personality." My very limited research confirms that that time is crucial to choices made from then on.

Adam laughs now as he tells me that he wanted to quit school to tour with a band "before there was a tour to go on!" He recalls that Judy was supportive of his musical ambition, but insisted on college as "a backup plan." He realizes how lucky he is that he grudgingly followed her advice, because it was at the New School where Adam met the other members of the yet-to-be-named X Ambassadors, Sam and Casey Harris and Noah Feldshuh. He joined them to play at campus parties and any other gig they could book. Before he graduated they had recorded and released several albums that drew the attention of other musicians and producers who wanted to work with them, Imagine Dragons in particular. Now he had a band to tour with. They opened for larger, better-known bands but built their own fan base as they went. These were bare-bones tours; they drove in a van and slept four to a room in cheap motels. They were paying their dues.

When they were booked as the opening band at the 9:30 Club in Washington, DC, I offered them the use of my suburban home there. I knew I would be in California at the time, so a perfectly comfortable three-bedroom house would be sitting empty. Not only did they accept my offer, but they sent flowers to thank me and to this day gush about how great it was to have a kitchen! And space! And more than one bathroom! They still haven't forgotten their "dues-paying" days. I think I have backstage passes for life. Having a front-row seat to a band on the rise is exhilarating. The last X Ambassadors show I attended was at the Fonda Theatre in LA in November 2015, when they displayed their newly earned first platinum record. Adam showed me their enormous, shiny new tour bus parked outside, which they planned to call home for most of the next year and a half. The advantages to having a tour bus are many. They can play and write together on the bus. And the familiarity the bus provides for Casey, their keyboard player, is particularly important. He is blind. Traveling to one unfamiliar hotel room after another must have been challenging for him.

With a tour bus to take them to many of the two hundred venues on their tour, and with their breakout hit "Renegades" topping the charts, Adam says, "Everything's changed for us." Now they have a larger crew and more obligations to do promos and interviews. "We're able to pay our rent and live more comfortably, but we're never home to enjoy that!"

Their stages are larger, their audiences greater in number, and their billing closer to the top. Adam recently posted a Facebook photo that showed him looking out at the throngs of almost a hundred thousand fans from the main stage at Lollapalooza in Chicago, where X Ambassadors opened for Jane's Addiction and the Red Hot Chili Peppers. He described the scene as "Amazing, surreal, crazy!" Adam recalls that four years ago, "when we played Lollapalooza for the first time, our time slot was at noon on Thursday on a tiny stage, a platform with a little sound system." And now this!

Judy understands the life-changing consequences of the choices we make. After she and Alan ended their twenty-year marriage, she knew she would need to find a more lucrative job than teaching dance in other people's studios. A friend offered her the opportunity to learn the real estate business, and a new phase of life began—with unexpected major shifts. The former dancer replaced her leotards, tights, and sweatshirts with professional clothing. She adjusted to new work behaviors, much more social interaction, and flexible hours. She was able to work while she cared for Adam and his brothers. She became a successful agent. (She sold me a house some years later.)

Another unexpected life shift occurred when Judy accompanied a group of friends to a local art show. As they were leaving, Judy caught sight of a familiar face, one she hadn't seen in thirty years—and that had been in Michigan. Mark Kahn and Judy had grown up in the suburbs of Detroit, where many in the Jewish community spent their summers at lakeside cottages. The Sandweiss and Kahn families were among fifteen families who gathered at Bass Lake each summer. Judy recalls having a bit of a crush on the older Mark. But she often went to summer dance camps and missed the lakeside vacations for several seasons, so she hadn't seen him for many years.

Mark still looked young, fit, and handsome. Sparks began to fly. He extended his stay in California to spend time with Judy and then invited her to join him and his son on a trip to Phuket, an island in Thailand. When they arrived at their beachside hotel Mark made a life-altering decision. A stickler for details, order, and neatness, he believed the brand new hotel seemed not quite ready; it didn't meet his expectations. So he changed their plan and booked them into an older, more established hotel a block away.

On the morning of December 26, 2004, Judy felt an earthquake, "a little bit of a shaker," she thought, having experienced them often in her Southern California home. When she went downstairs to breakfast, Mark's son announced that the hotel was preparing to evacuate. They watched CNN to see what had happened a block away and later viewed

Judy, the ballerina

With Judy in LA

the devastation they had miraculously escaped. Boats were dangling from trees, and remnants of tiki bars and restaurants were shattered and strewn everywhere. The hotel they had originally been booked in was gone.

It is remarkable that they escaped unscathed. The beach where Mark and his son had been scuba diving the previous day was wiped out. The devastation in Phuket resulted in 250 deaths, over a thousand injuries, and seven hundred missing people. They had been so close! They flew to Bangkok, where they would witness the funeral procession of a Thai prince who had been killed by the tsunami.

I have always believed that travel reveals and tests compatibility. Perhaps that was the case with Judy and Mark. He proposed soon after their harrowing journey, and they were married the following June. Despite several health crises this adventurous duo has traveled to many of Adam's shows, and Judy keeps her friends informed of the band's LA appearances. Because of that I have seen the X Ambassadors several times, starting in their early days, when they played in small, local clubs, and culminating in their current sold-out shows.

The band is known for great live performances featuring songs that top charts ("Renegades" and "Unsteady"). A recent collaboration with Tom Morello yielded "Collider," which became the theme song for college football on ESPN for the 2016 season. In the past few months they have made appearances on *Jimmy Kimmel Live!, The View, The Today Show, Good Morning America,* and *Ellen.* They have moved to LA with plans to get back into the studio. Adam hasn't lived in California since high school but looks forward to "trading New York for friends and family." He says, "I think I like New York so much because I leave it often!"

Judy, happy to have her son closer to home again, looks at the tradition of artistic expression that began with her family and continues with Adam. She is proud that he has found "that thing in life that brings you joy, that you find you're good at, that gives you your place in the world."

The dancer mom completely understands.

TOM MORELLO

Born: May 30, 1964, in Harlem, New York

Rage Against the Machine (1991–2000, 2007–2011),
Audioslave (2001–2007), Prophets of Rage (2016–present):
Guitar, vocals, harmonica, mandolin, bass guitar, drums, piano, banjo

Genres: Alternative metal, funk metal, heavy metal, rap metal, folk

First Album: *Rage Against the Machine* (1992)

MARY MORELLO

Mother of Tom Morello
(Rage Against the Machine)

FIFTY-NINE COUNTRIES, THE TITLE ANNOUNCES. A list then follows of all the places Mary Morello has traveled to or lived in. It's a prelude to the video Tom Morello produced to celebrate his mother's nineti-eth birthday. Next come tributes from a diverse international group of admirers. A photo of Mary with Chuck D of Public Enemy is accom-panied by a video of his wishes for her continued good health. Then Bobo and Sen Dog of Cypress Hill send greetings. These early founders of rap music are followed by more well-wishers: Perry Farrell of Jane's Addiction, Billy Bragg, Serj Tankian, Kid Rock, Gustavo Dudamel of the Los Angeles Philharmonic, and Yo-Yo Ma. Old friends from around the world send their love. Bono from U2 serenades her. The video ends with an extended greeting from Harry Belafonte, who praises her work in words and song. What a life this woman has led! Now ninety-two, she's still vital, marvelously interesting, and delightful to talk to.

Mary lives in a lovely cottage in the Hollywood Hills, next door to her son, who is an accomplished musician best known perhaps for his work in Rage Against the Machine and Audioslave. My house is only a few miles away, so it's an easy drive to meet the woman I've read so much about.

Mary was born in 1924 in Marseilles, Illinois, a small coal-mining town in the north-central part of the state. There, her Italian grandfa-ther opened a tavern, which her father later took over. The tavern was a central gathering place. Some came to play pool; miners and factory

Mary & Tom...

"Global Tourist Warriors"

workers came for a shot and a beer after finishing their shifts. Others showed up to talk about world affairs with the man who read the *Wall Street Journal* behind the bar every day. Mary's father knew everyone in town. Strongly pro-labor, he instilled in his three children the value of hard work and the need to demand fair treatment. Mary did not leave those lessons in her past. They fueled her passions for issues of social justice for the rest of her life.

Mary, her sister, and her brother were encouraged to succeed in school. It was easy for Mary. She was an avid reader and quick to achieve. Her consistent scholastic success led to scholarships to the University of Illinois, where she majored in history. After graduation Mary taught school ("I taught gym in a field!" she laughs) until she needed to return to Marseilles to run the tavern for a year after her father was injured in an accident.

Then the wanderlust began. When she was twenty-four she boarded an Army boat and set off for Wiesbaden, Germany, where she taught on a US Air Force base. It was 1948. Postwar Europe was not yet a tourist destination, and reminders of World War II were everywhere, but Mary and her adventurous American counterparts traveled throughout the continent on weekends and holidays. They would catch an Army flight to Paris for the weekend, take the train to Switzerland for Thanksgiving, or drive to surrounding German towns. Mary spent Christmas in Italy visiting the towns of her heritage. She traveled to Spain and Portugal, where an intriguing Spanish piano player convinced her to stay awhile. She taught there for a time.

Her next port of call was Asia. She secured a teaching job in Sendai, Japan, and to get there she booked a freighter, which became her favorite mode of travel. The camaraderie of the international crews and hardy travelers suited her well. While at sea Mary formed many enduring friendships with people from all over the world, some of whom appear on her birthday video. They were her kind of people, fearless wayfarers with broad worldviews.

I asked Mary where that adventurous spirit came from. She credits a high school teacher who was born in China of missionary parents. His tales of traveling the world fascinated her. She wanted to live the stories she had so enjoyed hearing. Her parents were encouraging, and she promised them she would never do anything dangerous. Later, as a mother, Mary imitated their permissive policies. Early discipline and establishment of trust laid the foundation for her son's later freedom.

When I spoke to Tom Morello shortly after my second meeting with Mary, he admitted that her unprecedented travels still amaze him. "There's nothing like it," he said. "It remains one of the great mysteries. It's not just that my grandparents were supportive. Where did the impetus come from? She is not able to explain it to my satisfaction." What he does understand, though, is that when he set out on his own risky path, Mary fully supported him. "She wanted me to be free, to follow my own North Star. So when I, with a Harvard degree in my pocket, announced that I was moving to Hollywood to play heavy metal music and start revolutions, she said, 'OK, fine. What day are you leaving?'"

After Mary returned to the United States from Japan, her keen interest in international affairs led her back to the classroom, this time as a student. She got a master's degree in history and African studies at Loyola University in Illinois. At a forum at Northwestern University she heard a speech by Tom Mboya, a highly regarded orator and one of the founding fathers of the new nation of Kenya. His eloquence piqued her interest in African affairs, so off she went again. After a six-week training course at Columbia University, she headed to a Kikuyu high school, where she had been hired to teach. It was there that she met and soon married Ngethe Njoroge, a young revolutionary who had played a significant role in the fight for Kenya's independence.

Shortly after Mary and Ngethe married, he was appointed to represent his new nation at the United Nations, so they moved to New York, where their son, Tom, Mary's only child, was born. The marriage was short-lived. Ngethe moved back to Kenya when Tom was eighteen months old. Mary and Tom found a small apartment in Harlem, where they spent a few happy years.

Their morning routine was a walk to a nearby park. After greeting their neighbors at the coffee shop, they headed toward the river, Tom in his buggy and Mary with her newspaper. My scenario includes Mary explaining world affairs to her toddler son, but she didn't recall that for me. On the way home Mary posted to telephone poles and building walls the NAACP and Urban League bulletins she'd stashed in the buggy. The friendships she made in her beloved Harlem continue to this day. Now when a Harlem friend is in need, Tom sends a local musician friend to help.

Mary's family convinced her to move back to Illinois to be closer to them as she moved on as a single mother. She agreed to the plan but wasn't prepared for the 1960s Midwestern version of racism that she and her bright, handsome biracial son would face. She set out job hunting with her stellar résumé but was regularly turned away. Finally, though, she secured a job teaching history in Libertyville, Illinois, a small village one hundred miles from Marseilles.

"I literally integrated the town of Libertyville," Tom told me. At the time, of course, he was unaware of the racist attitudes that forced their real estate agent to go door-to-door to secure approval of all the other residents before he and his mother could rent an apartment. Mary told him many years later that the agent's selling point was that Tom was not an American Negro but an "exotic" African child. Unfortunately the people who opened their doors to Mary and Tom slammed them shut again when he was old enough to date their daughters. "Then I could have been the Prince of Nigeria and no one would have cared," Tom says.

But Tom made lifelong friends in Libertyville and says that in many ways it was "an idyllic place to grow up." Green fields, Little League baseball, and riding his bike all over town are prominent memories.

Nevertheless, they can't erase the fearful others: the noose Mary and Tom found in their garage, or the Ku Klux Klan literature someone posted on Mary's classroom bulletin board. Tom and Mary were always aware they had to be careful.

When wanderlust struck again, "The Adventures of Tom and Mom" (title provided by Tom Morello) began. There were road trips to Yellowstone Park and Gettysburg and an eye-opening trip to New York City when Tom was twelve. But the greatest adventure was a summer in Europe when Tom was fourteen.

"It was a brokered deal," he admits. He had been reluctant to leave his friends, his dog, and his baseball team, but a bargain was struck when Mary agreed to add his requirements to the itinerary. He wanted to see the Loch Ness monster in Scotland, the Black Forest in Germany, and the Matterhorn on the border between Switzerland and Italy. Of course Mary would include his wishes in the travel plan. She says her philosophy of good parenting is quite simple: "Anybody in the world can raise a child well if they pay attention to him. That's my theory. You really have to listen, to pay attention."

So their first mother-son international adventure began. On her meager teacher's salary she booked flights on airlines no one had heard of and rented a car they would drive all over Europe. There were terrifying moments on icy mountain passes and miles added because neither son nor mother had a dependable sense of direction. After an extended visit to Paris they drove along the Riviera to Rome. They spent several weeks in London and once slept in a maid's room in a hotel that had no rooms left. Although Tom was able to cross off his three stops on the itinerary, there were times when, entirely sick of castles and ruins, he moped in the backseat and read *The Lord of the Rings*. Now, of course, he looks back fondly on that summer.

He couldn't know then how profoundly that foreign trek would affect his later travels. Now when he travels with a band, he's up early in the morning (so un–rock star like!), ready to visit all the places he's researched. "I've seen many of my rock brethren on tour," Tom says. "It doesn't matter whether they're in Cleveland or in Paris, their experiences are identical. It's the hotel, the gig, the after-party, the end. I became a global tourist warrior, brought directly back to that first trip to Europe with my mom."

Tom attended Libertyville High School, where Mary taught. My children and I had the same experience in Virginia. We piled into our blue Ford Fiesta each morning and set out for Thomas Jefferson High School, where Lisa was my student assistant and David my choice to deliver the morning announcements on the P.A. (often accompanied by certain-to-wake-'em-up heavy metal music). I was right down the hall if one of their teachers had a concern, and I knew their friends better than many parents know the friends of their kids. For the most part it was a very good arrangement.

Tom remembers the duality of the situation as well. On one hand Mary was able to assure that her scholarly son would get into the classes with the best teachers, like the history teacher he credits with helping to sharpen his worldview. On the other hand there were challenges when his mother, "not exactly tight-lipped, would reveal embarrassing details about my life. One year in her sophomore class, which contained potential dating partners [for me], she announced that I was circumcised! 'Mom! No! Stop!'" He laughs heartily at the memory.

Tom loved seeing his mother in the hallway and was in her African studies class his senior year. He did take advantage a bit, sometimes telling her that he wouldn't be in class that day—he'd be at home rehearsing with his band. She would sigh, "Oh, Tom!" and find a way to deal with the attendance card. Tom's love of music had started in junior high school. After a brief stint with the French horn he saved his money and bought a guitar. His mother bought him the requested amp to go with it. Predictably he hated the structure of lessons, but Mary found a program in a nearby suburb that included rock and roll as part of the instruction.

Mary was "the cool mom." Although she had never participated in any kind of music, she had gained a great appreciation for listening to it when she attended performances by the Chicago Symphony, where her uncle was a violinist for many years. Now her Libertyville house was the gathering place for all of Tom's friends and her basement the practice space for his band ("my noisy, unlistenable punk rock band," Tom calls it). He says he took her unconditional love and support for granted, thinking at the time that all mothers were like Mary. Later he learned how exceptional she was and now speaks of his "deeply kind, open-minded, fiercely protective" mother mainly in superlatives. "I thought everybody had a supermom like mine."

With Mary
in 2016

When it was time for college, Tom applied to Harvard, Northwestern, and Yale, schools that his research told him provided superior programs in drama and history. He had become interested in theater in high school and had been cast in many productions. He became the first person from Libertyville to attend Harvard. (He says, very humbly, that he was the only one to apply, but I don't believe that.) At sixteen, already self-identified as a revolutionary, he had considered moving to South Africa to join the military wing of Nelson Mandela's African National Congress. Instead, he decided to "arm himself intellectually" and believed Harvard was the place to do that.

At Harvard he formed a band, played gigs, practiced guitar for hours every day, and committed to his studies. He graduated with honors. He and his fellow musicians jumped into the van the Morello family had bought him the previous year and set out for Los Angeles, with Mary's approval. The van, by the way, is now in the Rock and Roll Hall of Fame in Cleveland. "I was happy he was going," Mary said. "If you have kids you want them to do what they want to do."

A year later, in 1987, Mary retired from teaching. She was sixty-three and had devoted twenty-two years of her life to her profession. Time to relax, perhaps? Of course not. Mary Morello began the next chapter of her life, a chapter I will call "Mary Morello, Activist." Her first cause was a fight for First Amendment rights and artistic freedom. The unknown retired teacher from a small Midwestern town firmly opposed the efforts of Tipper Gore, wife of then Senator Al Gore, and three other prominent Washington wives who founded the PMRC (Parents Music

Resource Center) in 1985. Appalled by the lyrics and video images of rock bands and the new rap and hip-hop groups, they came up with a plan to label and control the sale and distribution of albums they found unsavory. They wanted stickers to be placed as warnings on all albums deemed explicit or dangerous ("promoting an interest in the occult," for example). They urged record stores to put the "unsafe" albums under the counter, away from the eyes of innocents. They pressured radio and TV stations not to broadcast the music they objected to and even lobbied music executives to "reassess" the contracts of the individual artists and groups in question. They held Senate hearings and fomented heated debates.

Mary, not content merely to make a big protest sign or write a letter to the editor, founded Parents for Rock and Rap, a national anticensorship organization. During her ten-year tenure at the helm of the organization, Mary spoke to groups or interviewers or forums to combat what she believed to be an assault on free speech. She did radio shows with Ice-T, press conferences with 2 Live Crew, and appeared on *The Oprah Winfrey Show*. Please note: this was all before her son began playing with Rage Against the Machine. She raged first, determined to speak out for the protection of artists and their First Amendment rights. She was given the Hugh Hefner First Amendment Award in Arts and Entertainment for her efforts. And she made countless friends.

Tom recalled for me the time when Mary insisted he take her to see Ice-T's band, Body Count, play at a club in Los Angeles. She wanted to be in the first row, placing her in what her admiring and protective son described as a very dangerous mosh pit. He dutifully bore the blows of the ignited fans so that Mary could see her new friend Ice-T perform.

A few years after that Mary would be in the first row to see Rage Against the Machine, Tom's activist political-protest band. Over the years the band was together they were famous for their musicianship and the controversial issues they addressed, such as justice for the wrongly accused and countless international issues. They sold over sixteen million records in the relatively few years they recorded and once were introduced by Mary to an enormous arena as "the best f*#king band in the universe." That astonishing moment has been saved on the birthday video.

Mary traveled to Cuba four or five times with the Cuba Coalition, a Chicago group that worked to lift the US embargo against the island nation. She opposed the death penalty and worked with those who believed in the innocence of Mumia Abu-Jamal and hoped to have him removed from death row. She also supported Cindy Sheehan in her efforts with Iraq Veterans Against the War; together they produced many podcasts on which they discussed the war and its effects. She was interested in adult literacy and volunteered to teach in Salvation Army programs that promoted the cause.

Nowadays, Mary's life is still busy by other folks' standards but a bit quieter than it was. She goes to Tom's house every day to spend a few hours with Dee, Tom's wife, and their two young boys. On Sundays she joins the family when friends drop by to watch sports or just hang out. Mary volunteers at her grandsons' school two days a week to read to the pre-K students. She loves her time there. But she's still searching for more work, more opportunities to serve and "use my brain," she says. She remains an avid reader, enjoying books about world affairs during the day and more entertaining mysteries at night. And she's still rockin'! The night before our first meeting she was at the Staples Center to see U2 perform.

During summer vacation the whole family takes an annual trip to Libertyville, the place Mary still calls home. Tom's children enjoy being able to ride bicycles and roller skate on the flat Midwestern streets.

Making America RAGE again, 2016

They love visiting a cousin who has cows on his farm, and they are enchanted by the summer arrival of lightning bugs, a magical nighttime surprise to children who have grown up in firefly-free Los Angeles.

Tom continues to play his "concrete block power chords" (as David Fricke of *Rolling Stone* has called them) in the company of many of the musicians I have written about. He has played with my son, David, Zac Brown, Dave Matthews, Mike D of the Beastie Boys, and recently was joined by Gary Clark Jr., who plays on Tom's most recent record.

In 2016 Tom formed a new band, Prophets of Rage, with two of his Machine cohorts, Tim Commerford and Brad Wilk, as well as Chuck D and DJ Lord of Public Enemy and B-Real of Cypress Hill. They have collaborated on lyrics and music as their response to the political chaos of the 2016 national election and launched a "Make America Rage Again" tour. They hope to send a wake-up call as they play at rallies and venues large and small.

Tom is working on a solo album, too, but recently interrupted his studio time to play with X Ambassadors at Lollapalooza. In addition, he collaborated with them on the song "Collider," which was chosen as the opening theme music for ESPN's college football broadcasts in 2016. He never stops. His musicianship continues to amaze and inspire. And his rage continues to find words and to search for action.

After so many years of study and concern for global issues, Tom told me that Rage Against the Machine's greatest contribution "is the same contribution that Public Enemy and the Clash made to me: to not feel alone in my beliefs that the world should be different, and that I can have a role in changing it." A greater influence, however, has helped him appreciate that he was, as he says,

> *One of the luckiest ones in the world of arts and entertainment to have the supportive mom who shelters you from enough so that you're able to have that little space to create, even when challenged by economic or racial circumstances. It's the mother-bear protective nature that finds a way to buy you that fifty-dollar guitar, to give a basement where you can practice it, and to not harshly judge your choice of music over law or medicine. It gives you just enough wind in your sails to see what you might be able to do. For that, I owe 100 percent of my career to Mary Morello.*

VIGNETTE #12

FOO FIGHTERS

A one-man band. That's how Foo Fighters began. Dave Grohl—songwriter, singer, guitar player, bassist, drummer—on an anonymous tape that was sent out to a few friends.

It may have begun as an exercise in renewal. After Kurt Cobain's death, David and Krist played a show or two together backing other bands, but they knew they couldn't revive Nirvana. That was over when Kurt died. David, however, had more music to play and reunited with his old DC friend Barrett Jones, who had moved to Seattle to open a studio. In one week a concept became a tape with fifteen tracks written and performed by David. He put the name Foo Fighters on the label so it would appear to be the work of a band and sent it afloat.

Record companies came calling, and our wise friend the entertainment attorney Jill Berliner, the one who suggested I write this book, gave David a bit of life-changing advice. She encouraged him to start his own label and maintain ownership of all his work. He named his company Roswell Records and allowed major record companies to license his work from him. He has since built and operated his own studio and production company. See what happens to these kids who don't like to be told what to do?

"Food Fighters?" people asked me for years. "No, *Foo*," I explained, trying to sound patient. "From the World War II flying squadrons that thought there were UFOs waiting to invade European fronts." There are varying interpretations of the name, but all agree that *foo* was the mispronounced French word for fire, *feu*. That's really all I know about it. I wasn't consulted on naming the band, and that's probably a good thing. Weird as it was, Foo Fighters sounded a lot better to me than the names of some of David's earlier groups: Dain Bramage and Freak Baby. Band names mystify me. The Beatles, for example. Misspelled by young lads who were playing their guitars when they should have been doing their lessons? Or a word cleverly coined from the noun "beat"? Pink Floyd. What's that about? And Garbage! A beautiful singer with a top-tier talented band, an award–winning group. And they decided on Garbage? It's all beyond me. Foo Fighters will do just fine.

When the tape got a lot of admiring attention, it became clear that David needed to find a band. It's hard to go on tour with one person singing and playing all the instruments. He recruited bass player Nate Mendel and drummer William Goldsmith, both former members of the recently disbanded Sunny Day Real Estate, a band from the Pacific Northwest. He asked Pat Smear to be the guitarist. Pat had played with Nirvana for about a year and was one of my first favorites. It had surprised me to learn that the tall, sweet guitar player who danced while he played and laughed all the time had been a member of the Germs, a notoriously unsilly band, which had been famous on the West Coast punk rock scene when David was eight years old. Pat never seemed that much older than David. Even now, despite being the first Foo Fighter to have gray hair, he disguises himself as a much younger guy. And he's the first one I want a hug from when I go backstage. When William quit and David had to search for a new drummer, he asked Taylor Hawkins, who was drumming for Alanis Morissette at the time, for suggestions. Taylor suggested himself. I remember meeting him in Bryant Park at the after-party for the MTV Awards. He and David seemed to have an instant bond. A band was forming!

Perhaps the most significant decision David made was to step away from the drums and move to the front of the stage to be the singer, the face of the new band. He had sung harmonies in Nirvana and other groups, but he'd never occupied center stage as the lead singer. It was a brave move, yet it seemed almost natural. His voice is loud and clear—and he screams admirably, too. Someone once commented to me that my son is the only singer he knows who can shriek on key. As a bonus, his affable, unrehearsed banter between songs became something Foo Fighters fans would look forward to. A live Foo Fighters show is always much more fun than listening to a record. Every show is different, unpredictable. On a personal level, I never know when or why he'll mention my name or call me to the stage. Sometimes it's as a sweet tribute as he explains that the line "my sweet Virginia," from the song "Arlandria," is about me. Or he might tease about my comparing "For All the Cows" to Michael Franks's music. Such is the price of admission for a folding chair at the side of the stage.

Foo Fighters as a group was formed over twenty years ago. Since then, there have been some personnel shifts, the first of which occurred when

Pat got tired of touring. Franz Stahl, David's former Scream bandmate, filled that spot for a time, and then Chris Shiflett brought his masterful guitar licks to the group. Later, Pat tired of retirement and came back, joining Chris in the lead-guitar lineup. Keyboardist Rami Jaffee began performing with the band on an acoustic tour to support *In Your Honor*, a two-disc record that was half acoustic. He continues to play with them. He's classically trained and enormously entertaining as he swoops over the keys and bounces through the songs.

The band's first record was released in July 1995 and was well received by the press in the States and in Great Britain. Of course, there were endless comparisons to Nirvana, about which David would not comment. He'd wait it out, let his band stand on its own. I wondered if it would ever end—after their first Reading Festival? After the debut record sold two million copies? David seemed patient. I was annoyed for a long time. Why couldn't people see that a bona fide musician doesn't stop when life interrupts? He adjusts, re-forms, rethinks, but he must get back to the music mother ship. He knows that is where he belongs.

Now, eight albums and eleven Grammys later, the Foo Fighters are back in the studio, writing the next exciting chapter in their book of music. Over the years, I've met all the girlfriends, then the wives, and now the bevy of children. A few years ago the summer festival tour became the family festival tour, with all the attendant chaos and fun. David took his wife, two daughters (now there's a third), sister, and mother along. Taylor and his wife brought their daughter and son, who set up his own miniature drum kit onstage next to Taylor's and played along with him. Chris and his wife added three sons, who tried to keep order backstage and played with Nate's son, and Pat and his wife brought their little daughter. Two areas were set up backstage—one for children, toys, diaper changes, and nannies; the other for grown-up guests and associates—with the occasional crossover. In London the ladies, big and small, dressed up smartly to go to tea at the Savoy Hotel, where we saw a famous movie star enter the jackets-and-ties-only tearoom in his bare feet. We giggled politely behind our teacups. The children's playground was Hyde Park, and the fabulous London toy stores were a big hit. I often wonder what memories the children will keep of those big-bus cross-country tours that served as their summer "camps." Paris instead of archery, Prague rather than swimming lessons.

Foo Fighters l to r:
Chris Shiflett,
Taylor Hawkins,
Dave Grohl,
Pat Smear,
Nate Mendel

I'd be willing to bet no one has had as much fun on tour as I have. From their first Reading Festival, where I got to meet Brian May and Roger Taylor of Queen; to the Invictus Games, where I met Prince Harry; to the Fourth of July performance on the White House lawn; to the concerts at Wembley Stadium, where eighty thousand people (each night) screamed and I cried out loud. Meeting Paul McCartney at the Grammys and then having a small family dinner with him was a major highlight for this rock fan mother. He was exceedingly charming as we talked about children and music, and he brought me champagne! For about a year I inserted "when I met Paul" into most of my conversations until my friends insisted they'd really heard enough.

As time goes on and David continues to record and perform, my calendars fill with music events at tiny clubs and huge arenas in the United States, Europe, Japan, Australia. Every year there are surprises I could never have predicted. This year, being at the Academy Awards as David sang "Blackbird" while the giant screen behind him displayed the faces of the movie-industry greats who were being memorialized was unforgettable.

The journey that started with Scream and Nirvana continues with the Foo Fighters. When David says, "Come on! Go with us!" I no longer bound up the steps of the big tour bus, but I'm able to accept a helpful arm and hoist myself in. I continue the adventure with the band I've grown to love and with my most generous, loving son, who has made a big, wide wonderful world of music possible for millions of fans, a loyal band, his family, and one rock and roll mom who hopes it will never end.

VIGNETTE #13

WHAT'S A MOTHER TO DO?

Your child is bouncing off the walls. He loves noise, his own or that produced by bands with terrifying names. He never slows down. He goes full speed all day, wreaking havoc on your previously quiet home and trying the patience of his exhausted father, his disapproving grandmother, and even you, his last ally. His teachers report that he can't sit still. His attention span can't be measured because it doesn't seem to exist. He's politely disruptive. In other words, he seems not so much determined to cause trouble as to be naturally chaotic. He should probably be evaluated by the school "experts" so he can be labeled—as ADHD, learning disabled, or perhaps some new category—"placed," and dealt with.

But what you know, dear mom, is that this electrically charged product of your womb is an affectionate, thoughtful, funny, creative spirit. He loves to make you laugh. And you do. He wants to make you happy. And you are—until you have to answer to those others who think he's simply "out of control."

It's not going to be easy. But let me tell you a few things about your energetic child.

I. The explosive energy isn't likely to subside. You will need to acknowledge the energy and help your child channel it in healthy, productive ways until "hyperactive" becomes "hardest working," as it has with many of the rockers I've met. Dave Matthews's teachers complained of his lack of interest and focus, but his mother, Val, invited him to sit and paint with her, and now he designs his own album covers. Pharrell Williams's grandmother was exhausted by the nonstop child who "pounded on everything" and recommended a drum purchase. Still noisy, but focused noise that changed mayhem to music. My own son endured year after year of helplessly defeated teachers who were unaware that he was forming bands, writing music, and playing for audiences at twelve and thirteen. (They would have been amused to learn of the early gig that his junior-high band, Dain Bramage, booked at a senior-care facility less than a mile from the school. The boys made the unfortunate choice of including "Time Is on Your Side" in the set list.)

2. Despite the challenges you and your "handful" will face, more likely than not your child will bring joy to your life. Most of the musicians I've met are so happy to be immersed in music that they are wonderful company. I've learned to expect interesting, stimulating conversations and great humor when I'm with them. Perhaps because

they work collaboratively and appreciate the success they've earned, most of them share it with their parents and their children, inviting us to tour the world, stay in beautiful hotels, and meet people we read about in newspapers and magazines. Go on those journeys with them! You'll never be bored. And if you're as lucky as I've been, you'll meet Prince Harry, President Obama, and Stevie Nicks!

3. The maddening energy, if channeled, is likely to propel your child to create new paths and explore new territory. The curious, creative child may find an unprecedented way to contribute to society with ideas nobody has had and the confidence to act on them. In the end, he or she will have made a difference.

It gets complicated, of course. You may tire of redefining "failure," that painful part of the process of growth and change. Your unremitting search for a school, a program, or a teacher who can take a spark and create a fire may be fruitless. Many will counsel you to "put your foot down," to demand that your nonconformist child "toe the line."

But you aren't helpless. There are actions you can take.

I. Establish trust early. You'll need it. You may have to give your son or daughter more freedom than other parents would be comfortable with. Your child may find comrades outside your predictable neighborhood confines, and you will have to decide whether or not they're ready for that. There is no way you can know for sure, so you need to rely on trust. My son devised a method of keeping me comfortable when he needed to branch out to dangerous downtown Washington, DC, by calling me each time he changed location. "Hi, Mom, I'm jamming at Alan's house now. I'll be home by ten." That was all I needed to know.

2. Keep talking—and listening. Talk with your child about ideas, plans, worries about the future of the world, political views, neighborhood news, family goings-on, teachers, drugs. All of it. Talk in the car, around the table, sitting on the edge of his bed. Listen carefully to his voice, his views. And as old-fashioned as it may sound, I would strongly recommend face-to-face conversations rather than texts with clever emojis.

3. Buy that "different drum" your rebel has been marching to.

Or guitar or fiddle or trumpet. And don't expect him to love the lessons that come with it. He will probably want to do it his way. Don't expect to understand this. Also take him to hear all kinds of music: jazz, classical, rock, country, whatever you can find in your area. Don't try to enforce taste. Just let him know what's out there.

None of this guarantees that you'll raise a rock star, just a more fulfilled human being.

If the creative flame burns in another area, try to identify it and keep it burning. Your child's ingenuities may involve designing, writing, cooking, painting, engineering, or performing. Be open to all the possibilities. Along the way assure your child that you see an achiever, not the underachiever that others might suggest. The hope is that your support, nurturing, and determination will arm your child with the self-esteem necessary to further his development and eventually give birth to an inner voice, a self-guiding mechanism for making decisions and striking out in new directions. He will want to make you proud.

For further evidence of the extraordinary success of irrepressible, high-energy, creative iconoclasts, think of Geddy Lee, Dave Matthews, Adam Levine, Michael Stipe, Dave Grohl, and Pharrell Williams, among many others.

And ask their mothers how supremely proud they are.

SELECTED BIBLIOGRAPHY

"20 Best Debuts of 2013: HAIM, *Days Are Gone*." Rollingstone.com. www.rolling stone.com/music/lists/20-best-debuts-of-2013–20131210/haim-days-are-gone -19691231.

"50 Things You Didn't Know About Adam Levine." Boomsbeat.com. www.boomsbeat .com/articles/1372/20140318/50-things-you-didnt-know-about-adam-levine-hes -ambidextrous-has-adhd-and-is-a-yoga-lover.htm.

"500 Greatest Songs of All Time (Kelly Clarkson)." Rollingstone.com. www.rolling stone.com/music/lists/the-500-greatest-songs-of-all-time-20110407/kelly-clark son-since-u-been-gone-20110527.

"About Josh Groban." MTV.com. www.mtv.com/artists/josh-groban/biography/.

"Amy Winehouse Biography." Biography.com. www.biography.com/people/amy -winehouse-244469#synopsis.

"Amy Winehouse Inquest: Singer Drank Herself to Death." BBC.com. www.bbc.com /news/uk-england-london-20944431.

Barlow, Eve. "Haim Sisters and Their Parents Reunite 'Rockinhaim' for L.A. Charity Concert." Billboard.com. www.billboard.com/articles/review/6524008/haim-con cert-review-los-angeles-rockinhaim.

Barnes, Tom. "Rage Against the Machine Is Still the Protest Band Our Generation Needs." Mic.com. https://mic.com/articles/114316/15-years-later-rage-against -the-machine-is-still-the-protest-band-our-generation-needs#.

Beaubien, Greg. "Freedom Fighter: 71-Year-Old Mary Morello Vigorously Campaigns for Rock 'N' Roll's Right To Rap Freely." Chicagotribune.com. http://articles.chica gotribune.com/1995-08-23/features/9508230003_1_rap-group-censorship-live -crew.

Bell, Rebekah. "Zac Brown Wants a Whole Series of Music and Food Festivals." Tasteofcountry.com. http://tasteofcountry.com/zac-brown-band-music-food-fes tivals-nationwide/?trackback=tsmclip.

"Bergen-Belsen Concentration Camp: History and Overview." Jewishvirtuallibrary .org. www.jewishvirtuallibrary.org/jsource/Holocaust/Belsen.html.

Betts, Stephen. "Watch Zac Brown Band's Soaring Segue From 'Free' to Van Morrison.""

Rollingstone.com. www.rollingstone.com/music/videos/watch-zac-brown-bands
-soaring-segue-from-free-to-van-morrison-20150128.

Blatt, Ruth. "How to Breathe New Life into a Product: Lessons from Blues Artist
Gary Clark Jr." Forbes.com. www.forbes.com/sites/ruthblatt/2014/06/26
/how-to-breath-new-life-into-a-product-lessons-from-blues-artist-gary-clark-jr/.

Carey-Mahoney, Ryan. "Big Stars Honor America's Veterans." *USA Today*, November
12, 2014.

Catalano, Jim. "With New Album, X Ambassadors Aim for the Big Time." Ithacajour
nal.com. www.ithacajournal.com/story/entertainment/2015/06/23/new-album
-ambassadors-aim-big-time/29164631/.

Chappell, Bill. "NASA Holds a Cookout in Space: REM's Michael Stipe Sings for
Shuttle." NPR.org. www.npr.org/blogs/thetwo-way/2011/07/14/137847560/nasa-
holds-a-cookout-in-space-rems-michael-stipe-sings-for-shuttle.

Coleman, Miriam. "Pharrell Williams Marries Helen Lasichanh." Rollingstone
.com. www.rollingstone.com/music/news/pharrell-williams-marries-helen-lasi
chanh-20131013.

Collette, Doug. "Warren Haynes: The Timeline of Sco-Mule and Beyond." Allabout
jazz.com. www.allaboutjazz.com/warren-haynes-the-timeline-of-sco-mule-and
-beyond-govt-mule-by-doug-collette.php?page=1.

Cunningham, John M. "Miranda Lambert." Brittanica.com. www.britannica.com
/biography/Miranda-Lambert.

"Dave Matthews Biography." Antsmarching.org. http://antsmarching.org/bios
/DaveMatthews.php.

Davidson, Rebecca, and Jason Chester. "'My Husband Is Running from Me': Kelly
Clarkson Reveals Spouse Brandon Blackstock Is Laying Low Because She Wants
Another Child. Dailymail.co.uk. www.dailymail.co.uk/tvshowbiz/article-2908431
/Kelly-Clarkson-reflects-seven-months-motherhood-looks-difficult-pregnancy
-daughter-River-Rose.html.

Day, Elizabeth. "Growing Up with My Sister Amy Winehouse." Theguardian.com.
www.theguardian.com/music/2013/jun/23/amy-winehouse-growing-up-sister.

De Deyn Kirk, Kristen. "The First Mom of Music." Coastalvirginiamag.com. www
.coastalvirginiamag.com/October-2014/The-First-Mom-of-Music/.

Delancey, Morgan. *Dave Matthews Band: Step into the Light.* Toronto, ON: E C W
Press, 1998.

Dickey, Jack. "Taylor Strikes a Chord," *Time,* November 13, 2014.

Doyle, Patrick. "Gary Clark Jr.: The Chosen One." Rollingstone.com. www.rolling
stone.com/music/news/gary-clark-jr-the-chosen-one-20131224.

Doyle, Patrick. "Warren Haynes and Derek Trucks Leaving Allman Brothers Band."
Rollingstone.com. www.rollingstone.com/music/news/warren-haynes-and-derek
-trucks-leaving-allman-brothers-band-20140108.

Doyle, Patrick. "Tom Morello: Rage Against the Machine May Not Play Again." Roll
ingstone.com. www.rollingstone.com/music/news/tom-morello-rage-against-the
-machine-may-not-play-again-20121204.

Dunkerley, Beville. "Zac Brown Band's Spirited 'Homegrown' Is First Step in Global
Mission." Rollingstone.com. www.rollingstone.com/music/features/zac-brown
-bands-spirited-homegrown-is-first-step-in-global-mission-20150112.

Eddy, Chuck. "Lay It Down, Clowns!: The Beastie Boys Take Over?" Beatpatrol.com.

https://beatpatrol.wordpress.com/2009/04/03/chuck-eddy-lay-it-down-clowns
-the-beastie-boys-take-over-1987/.

Eliscu, Jenny. "Amy Winehouse: 1983–2011." Rollingstone.com. www.rollingstone
.com/music/news/amy-winehouse-1983-2011-20120723.

Eliscu, Jenny. "The Diva and Her Demons." Rollingstone.com. www.rollingstone
.com/music/news/the-diva-and-her-demons-rolling-stones-2007-amy-wine
house-cover-story-20110723.

Epstein, Dan. "Gary Clark Jr.: The New Hendrix Won't Stop Adventuring." Rolling
stone.com. www.rollingstone.com/music/news/gary-clark-jr-the-new-hendrix
-wont-stop-adventuring-20140630.

Eytan, Declan. "Pharrell Williams Becomes Co-Owner of Denim Brand G-Star."
Forbes.com. www.forbes.com/sites/declaneytan/2016/02/10/pharrell-williams
-becomes-co-owner-of-denim-brand-g-star/.

Fabian, Shelly. "The Zac Brown Band Biography." Countrymusic.about.com. http://
countrymusic.about.com/od/zacbrownband/p/ZacBrownBandPR.htm.

Fadroski, Kelli Skye. "X Ambassadors Hit the Road Like 'Renegades.'" OCRegister
.com. www.ocregister.com/articles/band-675121-ambassadors-harris.html.

Falcone, Dana Rose. "Josh Groban Teases New Album Details." EW.com. www
.ew.com/article/2016/01/11/josh-groban-new-album-interview.

Faughnder, Ryan. "Beats Music Completes a New Round of Funding." *Los Angeles
Times*, March 12, 2014.

Fell, James. "Lee's in No Rush to Retire." *Los Angeles Times,* August 1, 2015.

Fowler, Jacqueline L. "Living with Art in the Round." NYTimes.com. www.nytimes
.com/1978/04/13/archives/living-with-art-in-the-round-living-with-art-in-the
-round.html.

Frehsee, Nicole. "Amy Winehouse." Rollingstone.com. www.rollingstone.com/music/
artists/amy-winehouse/biography.

Fricke, David. "Best Young Gun: Gary Clark Jr." *Rolling Stone,* April 28, 2011.

Fricke, David. "100 Greatest Guitarists: David Fricke's Picks: 23. Warren Haynes."
Rollingstone.com. www.rollingstone.com/music/lists/100-greatest-guitarists-of
-all-time-19691231/warren-haynes-20101202.

Fricke, David. "The Battle of Rage Against the Machine." Rollingstone.com. www
.rollingstone.com/music/news/the-battle-of-rage-against-the-machine-19991125.

Fricke, David. "Michael Stipe on the End of R.E.M. as We Know It." Rollingstone.com.
www.rollingstone.com/music/news/michael-stipe-on-the-end-of-r-e-m-as-we
-know-it-20111129.

Fricke, David. "Artist of the Year: R.E.M.'s Michael Stipe on the Band's First Decade."
Rollingstone.com. www.rollingstone.com/music/news/michael-stipe-the-rolling
-stone-interview-19920305.

Friedman, Devin. "Pharrell Williams: The Man Who Never Sleeps." *Gentlemen's
Quarterly,* January 19, 2015.

Garbin, Patrick. *Images of Modern America: Athens.* Charleston, SC: Arcadia Publishing, 2014.

Gardner, Chris. "Pharrell Williams on Adidas Collaboration: 'I'll Never Be a Michael
Jordan.'" Hollywoodreporter.com. www.hollywoodreporter.com/news/pharrell
-williams-adidas-collaboration-ill-753967.

Garyclarkjr.com. www.garyclarkjr.com.

Geller, Wendy. "The Songwriters' Story Behind Miranda Lambert's Confessional 'Priscilla.'" Rollingstone.com. www.rollingstone.com/music/news/the-songwriters -story-behind-miranda-lamberts-confessional-priscilla-20150126.

Goodman, Elizabeth. "Michael Stipe Reveals R.E.M. Has Had 'Tough Ten Years.'" Rollingstone.com. www.rollingstone.com/music/news/michael-stipe-reveals-r-e-m-has-had-tough-ten-years-20070917.

Gotrich, Lars. "50 Artists Who Inspired Kurt Cobain." NPR.org. www.npr.org/2011/09/19/140487084/the-mix-50-artists-who-inspired-kurt-cobain.

Gottlieb, Jed. "Warren Haynes, 'Ashes & Dust.'" Bostonherald.com. www.bostonher ald.com/entertainment/music/music_news/2015/07/warren_haynes_ashes_dust.

Griffin, Verna. *Long Road Outta Compton*. Boston: Da Capo Press, 2008.

Grow, Kory. "Michael Stipe Talks Freedom Tower's 'Dark Nationalism' on 9/11 Anniversary." Rollingstone.com. www.rollingstone.com/music/news/michael-stipe -talks-freedom-towers-dark-nationalism-on-9–11-anniversary-20140911.

Grow, Kory. "Pharrell's Grammy Hat Could Be Yours for the Price of a Compact Car." Rollingstone.com. www.rollingstone.com/music/news/pharrells-grammy-hat -could-be-yours-for-the-price-of-a-compact-car-20140221.

Grow, Kory. "Foo Fighters, Beck, Zac Brown Band, Skrillex to Play Hangout Fest." Rollingstone.com. www.rollingstone.com/music/news/foo-fighters-beck-zac -brown-band-skrillex-to-play-hangout-fest-2015011.

"Heard on All Things Considered: R.E.M., R.I.P." NPR.org. www.npr.org/2011/11/16/142392387/r-e-m-r-i-p.

"Heard on All Things Considered: R.E.M. Members to Discuss Band's History." NPR.org. www.npr.org/2011/11/15/142361920/r-e-m-members-to-discuss-bands-his-tory.

"Heard on All Things Considered: The Story of R.E.M. Without the Greatest Hits." NPR.org. www.npr.org/2009/10/25/114117204/the-story-of-r-e-m-without-the -greatest-hits.

"Heard on Fresh Air: R.E.M. Become Part of Rock's Official History." NPR.org. www .npr.org/templates/story/story.php?storyId=7798722.

"Heard on Fresh Air: Pharrell Williams: Just Exhilaratingly Happy." NPR.org. www .npr.org/2014/03/06/286864627/pharrell-williams-new-album-is-as-happy-as -its-hit-single.

"Heard on Morning Edition: R.E.M. Tackles Songs of Faith and Revenge." NPR.org. www.npr.org/templates/story/story.php?storyId=88759457.

"Heard on Morning Edition: Pharrell Williams on Juxtaposition and Seeing Sounds." NPR.org. www.npr.org/sections/therecord/2013/12/31/258406317/pharrell-wil liams-on-juxtaposition-and-seeing-sounds.

Helmore, Ed. "From Spreading Happiness to Saving the Planet, the Rise and Rise of Pharrell." TheGuardian.com. www.theguardian.com/music/2015/jan/25/pharrell -williams-spreading-happiness-to-saving-the-planet-al-gore.

Hernandez, Raoul. "Gary Clark Jr.: The Chosen One." Austinchronicle.com. www.aus tinchronicle.com/daily/music/2013-07-26/gary-clark-jr-the-chosen-one/.

Holmes, Linda. "Pharrell Williams and the Power Hat." NPR.org. www.npr.org/blogs/monkeysee/2014/01/27/267017043/pharrell-williams-and-the-power-hat.

Holthouse, David. "Bottled Anger." Phoenixnewtimes.com. www.phoenixnewtimes .com/music/bottled-anger-6423546.

"How 10 Guitar Gods Got Started: 10. Gary Clark, Jr." Rollingstone.com. www.rolling

stone.com/music/pictures/how-10-guitar-gods-got-started-20131101/gary-clark-jr-0691921.

Hudak, Joseph. "Miranda Lambert Gives a Woman's Take on 'Bro Country.'" Rolling stone.com. www.rollingstone.com/music/news/miranda-lambert-gives-a-womans-take-on-bro-country-20140625.

Hughes, Hillary. "Gary Clark Jr. Will Be a Rock God Soon." Esquire.com. www.esquire.com/entertainment/music/a27248/gary-clark-jr-rock-god/.

Hunt, Kenya. "Pharrell Williams Talks Race, Black Women and Social Justice." *Ebony*, November 13, 2014.

Jennings, Angel. "'Straight Outta Compton' Moviegoers See a Painful Past, but a Happy Ending." *Los Angeles Times*, August 14, 2015.

Johnson, Kevin. "Parents for Rock and Rap." Theroc.org. www.theroc.org/roc-mag/textarch/roc-03/roc03-07.htm.

JoshGroban.com. www.joshgroban.com.

"Josh Groban Biography." Aceshowbiz.com. www.aceshowbiz.com/celebrity/josh_groban/biography.html.

"Josh Groban Biography." Billboard.com. www.billboard.com/artist/305237/josh-groban/biography.

"Josh Groban Biography." Biography.com. www.biography.com/people/josh-groban.

"Kelly Clarkson Biography." Biography.com. www.biography.com/people/kelly-clarkson-9542602.

Kershaw, Tom. "The Religion and Political Views of Josh Groban." Hollowverse.com. http://hollowverse.com/josh-groban/.

Kreps, Daniel. "Taylor Swift Recruits HAIM for Select 1989 Tour Dates." Rolling stone.com. www.rollingstone.com/music/news/taylor-swift-recruits-haim-for-select-1989-tour-dates-20150201.

Kronsberg, Matthew. "Zac Brown's 'Eat & Greet' Tour Serves Fans Grits Before Hits." Fastcompany.com. www.fastcompany.com/1792293/zac-browns-eat-greet-tour-serves-fans-grits-hits.

Laban, Linda. "Is X Ambassadors More than a Radio-Friendly Buzz Band?" Observer.com. http://observer.com/2015/07/writing-with-rihanna-scoring-commercials-get-ready-to-love-x-ambassadors/#ixzz3j7EX5aKA.

Leahey, Andrew. "Miranda Lambert Makes New Fan in Priscilla Presley." Rolling stone.com. www.rollingstone.com/music/news/miranda-lambert-makes-new-fan-in-priscilla-presley-20140612#ixzz3S4VkF75w.

Leahey, Andrew. "A Country Music Fan's Guide to Super Bowl XLIX." Rollingstone.com. www.rollingstone.com/music/news/a-country-music-fans-guide-to-super-bowl-xlix-20150128#ixzz3QtvSBJL6.

Levine, Adam. "ADHD Isn't a Bad Thing." Additudemag.com. www.additudemag.com/adhd/article/10112.html.

Lewis, Randy. "Stagecoach 2015: Miranda Lambert Has Gone from Opener to Headliner." LATimes.com. www.latimes.com/entertainment/music/posts/la-et-ms-stagecoach-2015-miranda-lambert-headliner-20150426-story.html.

Lewis, Randy. "Review: Miranda Lambert's Back in the Spotlight at the Greek, and Her Aim Is True." LATimes.com. www.latimes.com/entertainment/music/la-et-ms-miranda-lambert-greek-theatre-20160803-snap-story.html.

Lifton, Dave. "President Obama's Summer 2016 Playlist Includes Courtney Barnett,

Gary Clark Jr., Edward Sharpe + More." Diffuser.fm. http://diffuser.fm/president -obama-summer-2016-playlist/.

Light, Alan. "The Story of Yo: The Oral History of the Beastie Boys." Spin.com. www .spin.com/1998/09/story-yo-oral-history-beastie-boys/.

Littleton, Cynthia. "Protests Don't Rock Cleveland During RNC but Tom Morello Does." Variety.com. http://variety.com/2016/biz/news/republican-national-con vention-cleveland-tom-morello-prophets-of-rage-1201820852/.

Love, Bret. "Home Grown: Slow, Steady Steps to Stardom." Georgiamusic.org. www .georgiamusic.org/home-grown-zac-brown-slow-steady-steps-to-stardom/.

Manchester, William. *The Glory and the Dream: A Narrative History of America 1932– 1972*. Boston and Toronto: Little, Brown and Company, 1974.

Margolis, Lynne. "Gary Clark Jr. Goes 'Inside Arlyn Studios' with Willie Nelson." Americansongwriter.com. http://americansongwriter.com/2014/11/gary-clark-jr -goes-inside-arlyn-studios-willie-nelson/.

Matthews, Val. "A Postal Lament." Blogspot.com. http://civicsoapbox.blogspot .com/2010/04/postal-lament-by-val-matthews.html.

Matthews, Val. "Downsizing." Blogspot.com. http://hopeful-ink.blogspot.com/ 2010/10/downsizing-by-val-matthews.html.

Matthews, Val. "The Lost Art of Letter Writing." Blogspot.com. http://hopeful-ink .blogspot.com/2011/07/lost-art-of-letter-writing-civic.html.

McCormick, Neil. "Amy Winehouse: The Final Interview." Telegraph.co.uk. www .telegraph.co.uk/culture/music/rockandpopfeatures/8665516/Amy-Winehouse -the-final-interview.html.

McLean, Craig. "Josh Groban: I Like Making People Laugh—but My Music's Always Making Them Cry." Telegraph.co.uk. www.telegraph.co.uk/culture/music/rockan dpopfeatures/9926931/Josh-Groban-I-like-making-people-laugh-but-my-musics -always-making-them-cry.html.

Mettler, Mike. "After a Jeep Commercial and a Hit Single, X Ambassadors Plant a Lo-Fi Flag on VHS." Digitaltrends.com. www.digitaltrends.com/music/interview-x -ambassadors-singer-songwriter-sam-harris-2/.

"Michael Stipe Biography." Biography.com. www.biography.com/people/michael -stipe-9542550.

"Miranda Lambert Biography." Biography.com. www.biography.com/people/miranda -lambert-369610.

"Miranda Lambert Opens No-Kill Animal Shelter Redemption Ranch." Rollingstone .com. www.rollingstone.com/music/news/miranda-lambert-opens-redemption -ranch-20141124.

"Miranda Lambert Wins Best Country Album Grammy." Rollingstone.com. www.roll ingstone.com/music/news/miranda-lambert-wins-best-country-album-grammy -20150208.

Morello, Mary. "Guest Editorial by Mary Morello." Musicfanclubs.org. www.music fanclubs.org/rage/articles/microphone.htm.

Morello, Mary, and Cindy Sheehan. "The Mary Morello and Cindy Sheehan Show." Axisofjustice.net. www.axisofjustice.net/MM_072307.htm.

Moss, Marissa R. "Miranda Lambert, Equestrian." Rollingstone.com. www.rolling stone.com/music/lists/country-stars-secret-talents-20140919.

"NAMM 2015: Epiphone Announces Gary Clark Jr. Signature 'Blak and Blu' Casino."

Guitarworld.com. www.guitarworld.com/electrics-gear-news/namm-2015-epiph-one-announces-gary-clark-jr-signature-"blak-and-blu"-casino.

Newkey-Burden, Chas. *Amy Winehouse: The Biography 1983–2011*. London: John Blake Publishing, 2011.

Nika, Colleen. "Pharrell Announces Clothing Line for Women, Limited Edition Shoe Collection." Rollingstone.com. www.rollingstone.com/culture/news/pharrell-announces-clothing-line-for-women-limited-edition-shoe-collection-20111027.

O'Shea, Mick. *Amy Winehouse: A Losing Game*. London: Plexus Publishing, 2012.

Panzar, Javier. "Giving Back to Compton," *Los Angeles Times*, August 7, 2015.

Park, Andrea, and Anya Leon. "Kelly Clarkson Welcomes Son Remington Alexander." People.com. http://celebritybabies.people.com/2016/04/14/kelly-clarkson-welcomes-son-remington-alexander/.

Pareles, Jon, Jon Caramanica, and Nate Chinen. "Chipper Remnants of a Life Turned Sour." NYTimes.com. www.nytimes.com/2011/12/06/arts/music/from-amy-winehouses-archives-lioness-new-music.html.

Paul, Alan. "Southern Rocker Warren Haynes Mines His Folk Roots." WSJ.com. www.wsj.com/articles/southern-rocker-warren-haynes-mines-his-folk-roots-1437600377.

Payne, Chris. "X Ambassadors Detail New Album 'VHS,' Imagine Dragons Bromance in Track-by-Track Video: Exclusive." Billboard.com. www.billboard.com/articles/columns/rock/6612590/x-ambassadors-vhs-track-by-track-video-interview-imagine-dragons-premiere-exclusive.

Perpetua, Matthew. "Pharrell and Hans Zimmer to Consult on Academy Awards." Rollingstone.com. www.rollingstone.com/music/news/pharrell-and-hans-zimmer-to-consult-on-academy-awards-20111209.

Pollock, Lindsay. "Running with the Bull Market." NYSun.com. www.nysun.com/arts/running-with-the-bull-market/3899/.

Pond, Steven. "R.E.M. America's Best Rock and Roll Band." Rollingstone.com. www.rollingstone.com/music/news/r-e-m-americas-best-rock-and-roll-band-19871203.

Ro, Ronin. *Dr. Dre: The Biography*. New York: Thunder's Mouth Press, 2007.

Ryan, Patrick. "14 Things We Learned Talking with Sister Band HAIM." USAToday.com. www.usatoday.com/story/life/entertainthis/2015/02/05/14-things-we-learned-talking-with-haim/77598824/.

Ryan, Patrick. "On the Verge: X Ambassadors." USAToday.com. www.usatoday.com/story/life/music/ontheverge/2015/06/21/x-ambassadors-on-the-verge-renegades/71065710/.

Schilling, Mary Kate. "Pharrell Get Busy." Fastcompany.com. www.fastcompany.com/3021377/pharrell-get-busy.

Sidamed, Mazin. "Tom Morello and Talib Kweli Protest Against TPP as Fellow Stars Stay Quiet." Theguardian.com. www.theguardian.com/us-news/2016/aug/01/musicians-election-2016-tpp-tom-morello-talib-kweli.

Simpson, Leah. "We Were Madly in Love." Dailymail.co.uk. www.dailymail.co.uk/tvshowbiz/article-2273965/Josh-Groban-reveals-January-Jones-longest-relationship-hopes-similar-romance-soon.html#ixzz3jPN4Cczf.

Smolenyak, Megan. "10 Things You Didn't Know About Josh Groban's Family Tree." Huffingtonpost.com. www.huffingtonpost.com/megan-smolenyak-smolenyak/10-things-you-didnt-know-_1_b_1016372.html.

Sounes, Howard. "'Amy Said She Always Knew She'd Join the 27 Club': The Truth

About Winehouse's Death Wish and Why 27 Really Is an Unlucky Number for Rock Stars." Dailymail.co.uk. http://www.dailymail.co.uk/home/event/article-2360326/Amy-Winehouse-said-knew-shed-join-27-club.html.

Stipe, Michael. Speech inducting Nirvana into the Rock and Roll Hall of Fame. Rollingstone.com. www.rollingstone.com/music/news/read-nirvanas-rock-and-roll-hall-of-fame-acceptance-speech-20140411.

"The Parents of the Beastie Boys." Beastiemania.com. www.beastiemania.com/qa/beastieparents.php.

Tilles, Jay. "Interview: X Ambassadors Pleasantly Surprised by Jeep's 'Renegade' Campaign." Radio.com. http://radio.com/2015/07/10/x-ambassadors-renegade-jeep/.

Tschorn, Adam. "Pharrell Williams Joins Ranks of Fashion Icons." *Los Angeles Times* Marketplace. http://npaper2.com/marketplace/2015/05/01/s3/#?article=780632.

Tschorn, Adam. "'Happy' Days for Trendsetter." *Los Angeles Times,* February 8, 2015.

Van Noy, Nikki. *So Much to Say: Dave Matthews Band—20 Years on the Road.* New York: Touchstone, 2011.

Varga, George. "Gary Clark Jr. Discusses Transcending the Blues." SanDiegounion-tribune.com. www.sandiegouniontribune.com/entertainment/music/sdut-gary-clark-jr-interview-concert-preview-2016jul28-htmlstory.html.

"Venus Disarming Cupid, Gift of Hester Diamond." Worcesterart.org. www.worcesterart.org/exhibitions/remastered/venus-disarming-cupid-paolo-veronese/.

Wardlaw, Matt. "Warren Haynes Looks Back on 20 Years of Gov't Mule + His 'Unbelievable' Time with the Allman Brothers." Ultimateclassicrock.com. http://ultimateclassicrock.com/warren-haynes-interview-2014/?trackback=tsmclip.

Weiner, Jonah. "How HAIM's Three Geeky Sisters Became the Year's Coolest New Band." Rollingstone.com. www.rollingstone.com/music/news/how-haims-three-geeky-sisters-became-the-years-coolest-new-band-20131112.

Weston, Liana. "Meet X Ambassadors, the Brooklyn Indie Rockers Who Are About to Be Everywhere." Teenvogue.com. www.teenvogue.com/story/x-ambassadors-interview.

Williams, Pharrell. *Pharrell: Places and Spaces I've Been.* New York: Rizzoli International, 2012.

Winehouse, Janis. *Loving Amy: A Mother's Story.* London: Bantam Press, 2014.

Winehouse, Mitch. *Amy: My Daughter.* New York: It Books, 2012.

Wood, Mikael. "Dre to Release 'Compton.'" *Los Angeles Times,* August 3, 2015.

Woodroof, Martha. "Val Matthews Shares Her Thoughts on Poetry." WMRA.org. http://wmra.org/post/val-matthews-shares-her-thoughts-poetry.

Woods II, Wes. "Coachella 2016: Gary Clark Jr. Shines on Weekend 2." PE.com. www.pe.com/articles/clark-800908-coachella-stage.html.

Wyatt, Daisy. "Pharrell Williams—and His Hat—Are About to Play a Cameo Role in *The Simpsons.*" Independent.com.uk. www.independent.co.uk/arts-entertainment/tv/news/pharrell-williams-to-guest-star-in-the-simpsons-9997926.html.

Zeitchik, Steven. "*Amy* Follows Late Singer's Descent." *Los Angeles Times,* May 24, 2015.

ACKNOWLEDGMENTS

A book doesn't just happen. It can be complicated, especially when it involves mothers of musicians, located in many states of three nations, and the hundreds of businesspeople who represent them. What was I thinking?

When the idea dawned, I was in conversation with Jill Berliner, who insisted on translating an idea to pages of stories, to creating a BOOK! She was crucial to the first year, helping me outline the scope and dimension of my project, assisting in making the first connections with mothers who would meet with me, and accompanying me on the first three interviews, where she taught me a valuable lesson: talk less, listen more. She then had to return to her law-office duties, but remained supportive and helpful throughout. I am deeply grateful for her contributions and her friendship.

Gaby Skolnek and her cohorts at Silva Artist Management, experts in the music-business world, were helpful from beginning to end. Gaby advised and consoled in equal measure and was most valuable in making available appropriate resources.

My agent, Eve Attermann of WME, acted as an early reader and editor and provided guidance that helped to shape the form and direction of the book in order to match me with the right publisher.

Laura Mazer of Seal Press was a kind taskmaster and was patient with a first-timer who found the process of writing a book almost overwhelming. Her suggestions were key to discovering the critical aspects of the mother-child stories.

Michael Elins, a longtime friend, was the perfect photographer for the cover, flap, and Three Belles photos. He made the process a joyful one. Thanks, Michael.

Thanks to all the mothers who welcomed me into their homes and shared their stories and scrapbooks. I loved meeting these remarkable women, many of whom have become friends.

My most-valuable-player award must go to Joe Zymblosky, who became my "assistant" during phase one and immediately outgrew that title. He was involved in every part of the process: overseeing legal issues, accounting, travel, deadlines, transcriptions, research, contacting managers, and about a thousand other things. But even more valuable than his business savvy and perfectionism is the joyous nature of the man. Describing it will never do him justice. I'll just say that he has brightened every day he's been in my life, and I've treasured his assistance and his friendship.

Finally, the greatest thanks to my son, David, and daughter, Lisa. They insisted I carry a crazy idea through. No reservations, no doubts, nothing but cheers and support—and a whole lot of help with the process. I have always felt valued and loved, but never so much as during this challenging three-year journey to a book. *From Cradle to Stage* is for them, for Lisa and David, with all my love.